THE WISE WIFE

'Cause **Wisdom** Lasts Longer Than Botox!

MEGAN ANN SCHEIBNER

Character Health
101 Casablanca Ct.
Cary, NC 27519

ISBN: 978-0-9963270-9-1

To Steve: Have I mentioned how glad I am that you changed your mind about never dating Megan Pierce? Thanks for loving me so well!

To My Girls: Kaitlyn, Rochelle, Emma,
Molly, Baleigh, and Emerson.

Proverbs 31:29-30

Many daughters have done nobly,
But you excel them all. Charm is deceitful and beauty is vain,
But a woman who fears the Lord, she shall be praised.
May your greatest desire be to please the Lord and may you pass your wisdom on to our next generation of girls!

CONTENTS

INTRODUCTION

***Intimidating**: to make timid; fill with fear*

Writing a book about marriage and about living the life of a wise wife is intimidating! I've written many books for moms; that's fun! It's fun because my children are older and I can write from a vantage point of looking back fondly and remembering the sweet times. Even when I share my failures, it's all in the past and doesn't seem quite so "in my face." Because I see where they all are now, I can sit back and shine my Supermom crown! Ha-That's a joke!

Writing a book for wives though… that's tough stuff. Even though I've been married for 32 years, and even though I travel the country teaching a marriage course, and even though I've done years of marriage counseling it's still the hardest book I've ever had to write. Why? Because I'm still striving to live these concepts out! On a daily basis, God is meddling in my life and challenging me to be a wise wife. On a daily basis, I still have to make choices that will elevate God and my marriage and put to death my sinful appetites and well… Me. Like I said… That's tough stuff!

I'm convinced that if I was sitting across the table from you right now and we were sharing a cup of coffee together, you'd say that your heart's desire is to be a wise wife; a wife who brings glory to God by the way she lives out her role as a wife. I'm convinced that you just like me; want to get rid of anything that stands in the way of that goal. The problem comes as we try to figure out just how to do it. How do we live those lives of wisdom in the midst of busy schedules, burdensome bills, and barfing babies?

My greatest hope is that what you hold in your hands right now in some measure contains the answer to that question. This isn't so much a "what do I do" book as a "who I am" book. As we learn together how to live with our husbands in a respectful and relationally meaningful way, we'll see our marriages blessed and our personal lives changed. Change isn't easy, but when it's God-initiated; boy oh boy is it worthwhile!

The second reason that writing a book for wives is so intimidating is because I'm mindful of all the other authors who have gone before me. I think I must have read every "wife" book on the market in my quest to live biblically with Steve. Some of them have been wonderfully helpful, but others… not so much. They've run the gamut from legalistic lists of absolute "to-do's" that would qualify or disqualify me as a godly wife, to books that encouraged me to aggressively challenge my husband's right and authority to lead in our home. May I just say that neither

As we learn together how to live with our husbands in a respectful and relationally meaningful way, we'll see our marriages blessed and our personal lives changed.

extreme was biblical. I've read sweet, yet fluffy books that made me "feel" good about myself and harsh condemning books that just reinforced my already strong feelings of failure. I'm praying that this book doesn't fall into any of those categories! However, I do know that when we look into the Word of God and when we talk about biblical principles, you will be challenged. Some of you may want to shoot the messenger and I wouldn't be human if I didn't tell you that I hate that idea! However, I love the Lord enough that regardless… I must steward faithfully what I feel He would have me write. When fears of man (or in this case, women) tempted me to soften what the Word clearly indicates, I reminded myself of my life goal, loosely taken from Joshua 24:15:

"You do you, but as for me I want to live like Jesus."

My greatest prayer and desire for each of us as we work our way through these chapters is that no matter how challenging the concept or difficult the change, we'd do whatever it takes to "look like Jesus!"

In the back of this book you'll find two resources intended to help you on this Wise Wife journey. First, you'll find all of the scriptures for each chapter written out in their entirety. Throughout the text of the book, I'll refer to verses, list verses, and sometimes, include the entire verse. By putting all of the verses in the back of the book, I hope to make it easy for you to look at all of the scriptures and use them as an impetus for change.

The second resource you'll discover is a book study guide. This study guide is meant to provoke introspective self-examination as you read through the book. It can be used alone, or even better, in a small group of ladies. For those who are interested in going even deeper in their study, a separate Wise Wife bible study guide is available through Characterhealth.com.

I hope you find these resources helpful! Make this book a tool by underlining, highlighting, and writing little notes in the margin.

Before we get started let me just take a minute to tell you about myself. Here's some things you should know…

I'm the Heinz 57 of personality types. I'm an introverted melancholy who loves her personal bubble space and time alone. God, in His infinite wisdom, has given me a national speaking ministry and eight children who touch me All.Of.The.Time! (I consider it God's sense of humor) When I was a young wife living in Texas, my friends would line up every Sunday to hug me during the "Greet the visitor" time at church. They called it my therapy!

- My sense of humor is best described as warped. I'm one of those people who spend most of my life thinking, "If you knew half the things I wanted to say and didn't, you'd give me some credit!" I'll try not to shock you, but some things are just too funny not to share with you!
- I've been married to my college sweetheart for 32 years. He's my best friend, my colleague in ministry, and my partner in crime. No one makes me laugh more than him and he can still make me blush after all these years.
- I have eight children. Yes, I know where they come from. Yes, my hands are full. And **No**, I don't have the patience of a saint. (That last one is laughable!) I didn't set out to have eight kids, and in fact I didn't even babysit as a teen. God's plan was better than mine and I'm crazy in-love with each and every one of the "Scheiblets." I'm equally nuts about my "in-law" kids and don't even get me started on my five grandbabies. (Wanna see some pictures…)

- I didn't grow up in a Christian home and I didn't see a great marriage modeled before me. I came to Christ at the age of 20. After I replaced competitive athletics with competitive partying it became crystal clear to me just how desperately I needed a Savior. Trusting Jesus for my salvation is the best decision I've ever made and I shudder when I think where I'd be without him.
- I LOVE the scriptures! I have great mentors and older women in the faith who have poured into my life. However, everything I share with you comes directly from my time in the Word of God. My bible is my go-to source for my marriage, parenting, and every other area of my life. (Fun Fact: When I first came to know the Lord, I'd never heard of a concordance. So I wrote one myself! I made a list of every topic I could think of and began to record verses about that topic. Did I mention I might be a bit of a nerd? Imagine my surprise when I saw my first Exhaustive Concordance! Since mine took so much effort to write I titled it Megan's Exhausted Concordance.) The fact that God could turn a tomboy like me into who I am today is directly attributable to the transforming power of His Word.
- I love running, although now that I'm 54 I'm more like the tortoise than the hare. I love cooking, especially when I'm feeding a group of hungry teenage boys. There's no one more gratifying to feed than boys! I love tennis, and reading, and watching baseball. Go Red Sox! I daydream about organizational systems. Lovely,

color-coded, distinctively designed organizational systems with which I will change the world!

- I have lots of big dreams. Big Ones! God has already brought so many of those big dreams to life and I can't wait to see what He's up to next.

Finally, what's up with that title? That title is as much a reminder for me as it is for you. Like it or not, beauty fades. Proverbs 31, in verse 30, says this:

"Charm is deceitful and beauty is vain, but a woman who fears the Lord, she shall be praised."

I'm just like you. I spend far too much time looking in the mirror and fretting over the reflection looking back at me. The world says that beauty wins the day; God's word reminds me that wisdom and faithful living are all that count in eternity. We must "Acquire wisdom and with that acquiring get understanding." (Proverbs 4:7) When it's all said and done, our truest outward beauty will simply be a reflection of our beautiful Christ-focused inward life.

May God grant you the strength and understanding you need to truly become a Wise Wife.

CHAPTER ONE

IT'S NOT ABOUT THE WEDDING... IT'S ABOUT THE MARRIAGE

"We're all a little weird. And life is a little weird. And when we find someone whose weirdness is compatible with ours, we join up with them and fall into mutually satisfying weirdness- and call it love-true love."

Robert Fulghum

Do you remember the day you became a wife? I sure do! There I stood, Megan Pierce, the carefree Young Life leader, trapped in a gigantic white pouf ball! To be honest, when I looked in the mirror I didn't even recognize the girl looking back at me. I was a no make-up, sneakers and sweatshirt kind of girl. Now, here I was in a gown that made me feel like a toddler playing dress-up and, oh my gosh… wearing lipstick! Oh and not just any lipstick, either. My maid-of-honor, a beauty with red hair, had convinced me to use her lipstick… ***her bright orange lipstick…***

To make matters worse, when I'd informed the sweet ladies at the Bridal Shoppe that I certainly wouldn't be wearing a bra, (hey, the dress was lined) they'd done me a **huge** favor and installed a barbed wire monstrosity meant to give the illusion of a shapely bust line, which coincidentally was something I just didn't possess. I would have made any Viking mama proud. All in all, an auspicious start to my new life!

The wedding itself was an exhausting blur of relatives kissing me, strangers asking me endless questions, and just Too.Much. Touching! Quite frankly, weddings are an introverted, personal-bubble-space-loving girl's worst nightmare. We drove away from the reception and headed to our one night honeymoon. Steve was in Navy flight training and had barely convinced them to allow him to travel home to attend his own wedding; they sure weren't going to give him any extra time off. Because of his busy flight schedule, I'd "helped" him out and arranged for our romantic get-away. Let's just say that when a hotel has the word "Historic" in its name, you should have your doubts. After a quick dinner and a few minutes spent counting the wedding booty, (ok look, you know you counted your cash, too. This is a no-judgment zone, ladies!) We tumbled into bed exhausted, but successfully wed "until death do us part."

You probably won't be surprised to learn that I assumed that we'd gotten past the hard part. After the trauma of being a Bridezilla, I figured marriage just couldn't be all that hard. After all, I was an awesome girl (Steve told me so) and Steve was a handsome, dashing Navy pilot. What could go wrong?

I'm being totally honest when I admit this… After 10 days of marital "bliss" I was contemplating how I could ask my parents to let me move back home. There I was, stuck in Florida with an incredibly unreasonable and demanding husband. You won't believe what that man wanted me to do! He fully expected me to get up each and every morning and fix him breakfast! Are you kidding? I hadn't eaten breakfast in years. Besides, I'd just graduated from college and I had every intention of taking the summer off! Breakfast Chef just wasn't a title I was prepared to accept. I dug in… He dug in… We were miserable!

I still can't reread that paragraph without blushing. Can you believe it? I was a Christian who claimed to love the Lord. I'd spent all of my spare time in college eagerly serving high school students through the ministry of Young Life and yet, here I was stubbornly refusing to serve my husband, who by the way, I'd just pledged to love, honor, obey, etc., etc., etc…

Obviously, I had a lot to learn about being married and about pleasing both my Lord and my husband through my marriage. Although I eventually caved in and began to make breakfast for my Steve, (more about that in a later chapter) I still didn't have the faintest idea what it meant to be a wise wife, a wife who had captured her husband's heart because of her wholehearted devotion to glorifying God through loving him well.

It wasn't that I didn't want to learn; I just didn't know where to start. Which brings us to the driveway of my very first ladies bible study. We'd obediently begun to attend a local church as a married couple and on our very first Sunday there they announced a new "Wives Bible Study." This was it! The answer to my dilemma! I was convinced that **now** I'd learn how to be a wise wife and I'd learn it *faster than anyone else*!

There's something else you should know about me. Those of you who have heard me teach will already know this. I do everything fast! I drive fast, I talk fast, I clean fast, I cook fast, I read fast… You get the picture. Honestly the only thing I don't do fast is fall asleep and that's only because my brain is speeding fast, faster, fastest!

I didn't want to wait to become a wise wife. I didn't want to waste another day in marital mediocrity. I wanted to be that gloriously wise woman and I wanted to be her now, now, now! With that thought in mind, I sped to the home of the bible study leader. Literally. Like, I sped through her neighborhood and right past the stop sign at the corner of her road. Before I could ever meet the sweet ladies in my new bible study, they had the privilege of watching me as I met the "kind" police officer blocking the end of her driveway. That's me!

Fortunately, time and age and hopefully, maturity, has taught me to slow down and think. I still want results quickly, but I've learned that when it comes to growing in my walk with the Lord, He isn't looking for fast and shallow, but instead He wants me to grow carefully and deeply.

The same is true when it comes to becoming a wise wife. Wisdom doesn't happen overnight. It takes time! It also takes work, patience, prayer, and a commitment to change. I've been married for 32 years now. Steve still tells me I'm awesome, (and I still think he's handsome and dashing!) but thankfully, I'm not that same girl he married. God has taught me, and corrected me, and molded me, and changed me. That's not to say I've arrived... God's certainly not finished with me yet! However, I can look back over these past 32 years and see who I was then and know that because of Christ, I'm someone different now.

Wisdom doesn't happen overnight. It takes time! It also takes work, patience, prayer, and a commitment to change.

Quite frankly, I've had some wonderful mentors in my life; godly women who pointed me to Christ and didn't hesitate to challenge my preconceived notions of what it meant to be a wise wife. They were never afraid to give me a well timed kick in the pants and I'm so thankful for those women! However, almost everything that I've learned about being a Christian wife, and in particular, Steve's wife, comes straight from the Word of God. I'm absolutely, 100% convinced that God's Word has all that we need in order to know exactly how to glorify Him in each of our individual marriages. It's His Word, His precepts, and His commandments that we'll be studying in these pages and you can trust that He'll use those things to change your life!

Are you ready to work hard? Are you ready to be challenged to take your role as a wife to the next level? Are you ready to be changed in order to look more like Jesus and to bring more of Him into your interactions with your husband? If so, let's go! Slow and steady, we're on our way to becoming a Wise Wife.

CHAPTER 2

MEN AND WOMEN: THERE REALLY IS A DIFFERENCE

"You keep using that word. I don't think it means what you think it means."
Inigo Montoya-The Princess Bride

I don't know if you've ever noticed this, but men are reeaallyy different than women! Before I was married and moved in with my own man, I'm not sure I was so aware of the differences. Now after three decades of marriage and as the mother of four sons, there is no doubt in my mind… these guys just aren't like me! They don't think like me, act like me, react like me, and they certainly don't smell like me. (Did I mention four sons and baseball, soccer, and track socks?).

That male/female difference is part of what makes learning to be a wise wife so complicated. We come into marriage expecting our spouses to respond to things the way we would. (Reasonably, of course) When they don't respond the way we expect, we're just shocked. After all, they had no flaws when we were engaged and if they did have some tiny, miniscule, almost imperceptibly slight imperfection, we just knew that **We Could Change Them**. What a surprise when our malleable, eager to please fiancés suddenly become men with a mind of their own who just aren't willing to always see things our way.

I want to focus on that whole, "I can change him," paradigm for just a minute. That truly is the prevailing thought of our culture. Sitcoms and movies make light of the fact that young women believe that they can persuasively transform their boyfriend into the man of their dreams. Girls stay in ungodly and unhealthy relationships simply because they believe that they somehow have the power to change the young man to whom they're attached. Women walk down the aisle, disregarding the wise counsel of family and friends, because they believe that once they have the title of "wife," they'll have more leverage to bring about transformation in their new husband. The truth is this… it just doesn't work that way!

It is God that brings about change in a young man's life. It is the Holy Spirit who brings conviction into their heart. It is a transformative relationship with Jesus Christ that sparks the desire to become more like the Savior. There is no man who will be changed by the continual nagging or well-meaning correction of the woman in his life!

In other words, it's time to give it up ladies! You can pray for your husband and you can model sacrificial, Christ-like behavior

It is a transformative relationship with Jesus Christ that sparks the desire to become more like the Savior.

for your husband, but you cannot change him. It's a waste of your time. Instead, why don't we spend those precious hours working on us? Let's focus on learning to live as godly and Christ centered wives. Let's focus on serving sacrificially instead of nagging negatively. You can't change him, but you can, through the working of the Holy Spirit, change you!

I can't give you any guarantees, but as your husband sees you growing and changing to become a wise wife, hopefully he'll desire to grow and change as well. This isn't a "You do these three things and God will bless you with ______" book, but what I've seen through many years of counseling lots of women is that when a wife diligently strives to live like Jesus, she will see changes in her marriage. It's not always as complete or quick a change as she'd like to see, but God is aching to bless our obedience and He blesses us by showing us even small, incremental changes.

So, now it's all about that change. We're certainly not going to change to become more like our husbands. (I'm not even sure that's possible!) However, as we strive to understand what makes them think, act, and process differently than us, we can then make biblical and proactive changes in our own lives that will help us become the wives they deserve. Wait, let me change that...we'll be the wives God calls us to be...whether they deserve it or not!

Men and Women: What's the Big Difference?

Dr. Emerson Eggerichs, in his life-changing book, Love and Respect, explains the difference between husbands and wives like this: He contends that men desire respect and they base their actions toward their wives according to how respected they feel. Women, on the other hand, desire love. When we feel loved, all is well. However, when love is missing, well, the old adage, "hell hath no fury..." probably applies here.

Dr. Eggerichs is brilliant! I'm not kidding. Where was this guy when I was 22 years old and stubbornly refusing to make breakfast? We women try to be wise wives by loving our husbands the way we would want to be loved. Don't get me wrong. Our husbands certainly don't hate receiving love from us, (who would?) but they don't perceive love the same way they perceive respect. The love is nice, but if the respect is missing they still feel "unloved." We can double down and try to love them even more, but the results will still be the same. Love, without respect, will leave our men unfulfilled, unhappy, and eventually, distant and frustrated with us, and we won't even know why.

The problem is compounded by the fact that men and women view respect very differently. Things that I could jokingly say to another woman that would send us both into spasms of laughter can seem disrespectful to my husband. If Steve doesn't notice all the things I do for him, (let's be honest, I do so much how could he **ever** possibly notice them all?) I don't necessarily feel disrespected, but when I fail to show gratitude to him, he does feel disrespected. When Steve comes up with a plan and I fine-tune that plan to be "helpful," he doesn't feel helped; he feels disrespected.

The list of things that to me are no big deal, but that to him, as a man, are disrespectful goes on and on. For years, he tried to communicate his frustration to me. He would say that he felt disrespected, but because my actions didn't *seem* disrespectful to me, I flat out told him he was wrong. As you can imagine, our arguments became circular disagreements with him unlovingly accusing my motives and me disrespectfully rationalizing my behavior.

Dr. Eggerichs likens this cycle to a hamster on a wheel. He says that the more the husband feels disrespected, the more unloving he will be. This in turn causes the wife to feel unloved and she will treat her husband even more disrespectfully. Of course, a disrespected husband will respond with unloving words and actions, which causes the unloved wife to disrespect him even more vehemently. And on and on the wheel spins. Dr. Eggerichs calls this spinning the "Crazy Cycle," and as someone who has been there, trust me, it's Crazy!

Stopping the Cycle of Craziness

So, how can we break the cycle? Is it possible to stop the spinning and get off of the hamster wheel? I believe it is. All it takes is one spouse who is willing to humbly change their reactions. A husband who chooses to respond lovingly, in spite of feeling disrespected, can be a cycle-changer. By the same token, a wife who refuses to respond disrespectfully despite her husband's unloving words or actions can stop the spinning and change the entire direction of the marriage.

Since you're the one reading this book, I'm going to assume that you're prepared to be the cycle-stopper in your home. Stop!! Read that sentence again. Let me remind you once more; this

In our feelings-driven culture, the idea of changing in order to be a wise wife for a husband whom we may feel just doesn't deserve us is foreign at best and horrifying at the worst.

isn't about changing your husband so that he'll stop the crazy cycle! You can't. It doesn't work. Give it up. This is about you changing in order to please God, glorify Christ, and learn to live wisely as a wife.

In our feelings-driven culture, the idea of changing in order to be a wise wife for a husband whom we may feel just doesn't deserve us is foreign at best and horrifying at the worst. Why in the world would we do it? Trust me! There's a great reason to make that choice and it has nothing to do with you, your husband, or even the joy of your marriage. Those are all after thoughts, simply areas that will benefit from the greater good you achieve through making the choice to change. I'm going to ask you to put aside your feelings, (even if it's just for the moment) and to instead elevate the virtues of honor, courage, and commitment as you continue reading this book. Let's pray for soft, teachable hearts and let's see what God wants to do in our lives.

With that change in mind, we'll spend the remainder of this chapter discussing exactly what it means to respect our husbands. Then the rest of the chapters will present practical ways that we can put that respect into action each day. It's one thing to have the head-knowledge of what respect "looks like," but it's quite another thing to live it out on a daily basis.

Don't Say I Didn't Warn You

Let me warn you. Sometimes, you're going to feel like I'm meddling. Maybe even meddling a lot. Sorry about that, but I wouldn't be a good teacher if I didn't meddle with the status quo. Trust me when I say that I'll never share a hard truth that God hasn't already used to meddle in my own life. I'm going to try to be vulnerable and transparent in these chapters. I'll share my successes, (yippy!) but I'll also share my failures. I'm convinced that often we learn as much, if not more, from our failures as we do from our successes.

Some of the changes you are going to have to incorporate will be easy peasy, but others… not so much. Because change is hard and we all need to relax and exhale sometimes, I'm going to throw in just a few light-hearted chapters. You'll recognize them by this title, "What The Heck!"

What the heck is my "go-to" phrase for understanding life's little quirks. When I can't find my glasses… What the heck! When the checkbook won't balance… What the heck! When one of my kids does something totally out of the norm… What the heck! As one of my favorite television characters, Abby Schuto from NCIS says, when things are just "hinky"… What the heck! (I use this statement so often that my husband has threatened to put it on my gravestone. Of course it will be followed closely by: Where are my glasses! I forgot my phone! Did I turn off the iron? Or any other of my usual neurotic and panicked exclamations of alarm.) Ladies, men and the way they think definitely falls into the What the Heck category and I'll be using those chapters to highlight some incredibly male thinking.

I'm going to ask your grace to be just a little "snarky" and maybe even a tad irreverent in the What the Heck chapters. Sometimes, we just need to laugh about the differences between our husbands and us. I'll probably just be saying what you're already thinking, but you won't have to feel guilty about thinking it. And in case you're wondering, I have Steve's permission to "let 'er rip!"

R*E*S*P*E*C*T

Henri Frederic Amiel said this about respect:

"There is no respect for others without humility in one's self."

If we're going to learn to respect our husbands, we're going to have to get past the notion that they need to change their opinion concerning what is and isn't respectful. It takes humility to admit that our way of thinking and reacting isn't necessarily the only way of thinking and reacting. At times, we can both be right and just agree to disagree, but other times, we're just plain old wrong! I'm going to ask you to put to death any preconceived ideas you have about how your husband *should* feel about your actions, and to instead pray for a teachable and humble heart that truly desires to understand how he *does* feel about your actions toward him.

Sometimes, it's a hard pill to swallow that our husbands aren't owed our respect because of the things they've done to earn it. Rather, they are to be respected by us simply because of the position in which God has placed them in our marriage. In both I Corinthians and the book of Ephesians, God lays out the order of authority in the family. In both sections of scripture we are told that God is the head of Christ, just as the husband is the head of the wife.

This headship isn't a position of superiority. We are not inferior to our husbands in the same way that Christ is not inferior to God, the Father. Instead, this order is a picture of administrative order. We fill different roles and because of that we hold different positions of authority in our marriage. We are, in fact, honoring God when we choose to show respect to our husbands simply because of where God has placed them in our marriages.

My first interaction with this concept of "unearned" authority happened when Steve was a newly commissioned officer in the

Navy. As an Ensign, although he was the lowest ranking officer on base, he still outranked every enlisted man. One night, he and I bumped into his old drill instructor, Master Sergeant Fleger. Master Sergeant Fleger was a sight to behold. This marine was a finely chiseled specimen of a man with an intimidating scar running right down his cheekbone. Steve was scared to death of the man, but quite frankly, I found him *very attractive*. He was a decorated veteran of the Vietnam War and at least 20 years older than us. Steve, on the other hand, was a skinny 23 year old with no real-life experience other than his time in Aviation Officer Candidate School.

As he walked toward us, I watched as this rock of a man lifted his right hand and saluted my husband. It just felt wrong! Here was a man who oozed competence and experience. He was a warrior worthy of respect, but yet, he saluted my husband. For me, it was unfathomable.

Why did Master Sergeant Fleger salute Steve that day? It certainly wasn't because Steve had earned his respect. It wasn't because Steve had committed any notable acts of valor that required Master Sergeant Fleger's salute. The truth of the matter was this: Master Sergeant Fleger wasn't saluting Steve; he was saluting the insignia on Steve's uniform.

Even though Master Sergeant Fleger had more experience, even though he'd proven his valor, even though he'd served in combat overseas… He was still an enlisted man and my husband was an officer. Master Sergeant Fleger made the choice to salute Steve because he understood what the insignia on Steve's shoulder stood for and he honored that reality.

In the military, officers are the ones to lie out the plan and make the strategic decisions. They are given the authority to invade or retreat, deploy or return home. They make the decisions and they answer for the consequences caused by those decisions. Enlisted soldiers and sailors are the ones that carry out the decrees that the officers have made. Under the authority of the officers above them, brave enlisted members "make it happen!" Without such an authority structure, the military would be anarchy. Each member would fight to be the one in charge and nothing would be accomplished. The enemy would have free reign as infighting destroyed the squadrons and battalions. In the end, we would fall to defeat and our enemies would stand victorious.

It's the same in marriage. Our husbands wear an insignia on their shoulders, an invisible insignia placed there by God. In His sovereignty, the God of the universe has placed the mantle of responsibility squarely on the shoulders of our husbands. With that position of authority comes the burden of accountability. They will answer to God for their decisions, their actions, their responsibilities, and ultimately their leadership. Honestly, I wouldn't want their job; the stakes are too high and I'd be afraid of failing!

It's Your Choice

As wives, every day we face the same decision that Master Sergeant Fleger faced. Will we willing choose to subordinate ourselves to our husbands simply because of God's authority structure? Or, will we demand that they earn our respect? Will we try to wrestle control

Choosing to respect our husband has too often been portrayed as a woman's weakness.

from them? Will we second-guess and judge their every decision? If those are the choices we make, our homes will be anarchy, our families will be the casualties, and in the end, Satan will win.

Choosing to respect our husbands has too often been portrayed as a woman's weakness. We are only weak when we are forced into the position of having no choice. When we willingly, (dare I say eagerly) choose to subordinate ourselves for the good of our marriages and the glory of God, we are powerful! When we respect our husbands, electing to honor them when they haven't earned that honor, we are powerful! When we respectfully stand beside them in the aftermath of a bad decision on their part and refuse to point a finger of blame, we are powerful! As we respect our husbands, out of reverence for our God, we become culture-changers and my dear sisters… That's Powerful!

I realize you may have been told otherwise, but my friends, no one can force you to respect your husband. You have the freedom to make that choice! In the same way, you have the freedom to choose differently. You can choose to disrespect, dishonor, and do it your way. Again, you're free to make that choice, you don't however have the freedom to choose the consequences of your choices.

I'll be frank, without an eternity-minded goal for our marriages, choosing to respect a man who sometimes doesn't deserve that respect is incredibly difficult. If our marriage is all about us and what we get in return for our actions, we'll struggle and fail when it comes to the area of respect. However, if our goal is to bring glory to God regardless of our circumstances, what our husbands do to earn our respect will be secondary to our primary goal of honoring God through our own actions.

In I Corinthians 10:31, we are reminded that in whatever we do, whether eating or drinking or anything else, we are to bring glory to God. It's interesting to me that the Apostle Paul picked two ordinary, mundane activities to reference as he spoke of glorifying God. Be honest, don't you eat and drink every day? I do! It just happens. Other than the effort involved in planning our meals, (I am the mom, after all) eating is just one of those everyday occurrences in my house. Here's what I think Paul was trying to communicate to us. If we can bring glory to God in something as everyday and boring as eating and drinking, then we can *certainly* bring glory to God in those big areas that take forethought and planning.

There are times that respecting Steve takes every ounce of forethought and planning I can muster! Don't get me wrong. My husband is a natural born leader. He is the hardest, working man I know. He loves the Lord, he loves our kids, and he loves me. But sometimes...! Sometimes he just doesn't listen to me. Sometimes he just plows ahead and doesn't see the obvious (to me anyway) consequences. Sometimes he doesn't embrace my clearly (again, to me) superior plans.

Sometimes he just isn't somebody I feel like respecting at that moment, but my choice is still the same... I must respect him because my greatest desire is to glorify God in everything that I do. Does that make sense to you? Quite frankly, what Steve does and the choices he makes on any given day aren't my issue. The issue is my commitment to glorifying my Heavenly Father. Trust me, the God of the Universe is more than big enough to work in

Your marriage is a ministry and God blesses those who minister for Him.

my husband's life. When it comes to me and the choices I make regarding respecting that man He's given me… God is totally and completely and only focused on my choices, my obedience, and my relationship with Him.

When I choose to glorify God through respecting my husband, the most wonderful thing happens. My God is magnified! Literally that means He is made to look bigger to a watching world. A wife that doesn't respect her husband, or who only respects him when he's clearly earned her respect, is nothing new. Our world is full of wives like that! But a wife that chooses to respect her husband, regardless of whether he obviously deserves that respect or not, will earn the right to be heard with her friends and family members. That's the woman I want to be! That goal reminds me that my marriage is so much bigger than just Steve and I; it's a supernatural vehicle to transport those I love into the very presence of God.

We can't all be foreign missionaries. We can't all be teachers or bible study leaders. However, we can all have a ministry. When you willingly choose to show honor and respect to your husband, you are a missionary to everyone in your circle of influence. Whether it's your sister, your best friend, your neighbor, or the cashier at the grocery store… You can make a difference. God is glorified as you honor Him by respecting your husband. Your marriage is a ministry and God blesses those who minister for Him!

Preparing To Be Successful

So on the hard days, how do we maintain that attitude of respect when every fiber of our being is aching to respond poorly and assert our own superiority? Well, we certainly can't just stick a geranium in our hat and plaster a "respectful" smile on our faces. The Christian life has never been about "faking it until you're making it." The only way to walk obediently when the road is crooked and our path is full of potholes is to be spiritually prepared for those days so that we aren't taken by surprise.

The scriptures, especially in the book of Proverbs, warn us about two types of snares that can catch us up and cause us harm. The first type of snare is the snare we don't see. Imagine you're walking down a path and suddenly your foot is caught in a tree trap and you're dangling upside down trying to figure out what just happened. That's a trap you didn't see, you couldn't avoid, and now, you must find a way to escape. I'll be honest with you. There are days when it comes to showing my husband respect that I get caught up in that type of trap. I don't see a problem approaching and in the quickness of the moment, I respond disrespectfully. Just that quickly we can go from peaceful and loving to frustrated and hurt. When that happens there is only one biblical escape from the trap. That escape is the reset button of seeking forgiveness. We'll talk about that more in the last chapter, but for now, may I encourage you to be quick to humble yourself, admit your failure, and seek forgiveness? The only thing it will cost you is your pride and isn't honoring God and loving your husband worth more than holding on to your stubborn pride and self-preservation?

The second trap is different though. This trap is found in Proverbs 22:3 and again in Proverbs 27:12. In both of these passages we are told that the wise man (or woman, in this case) sees the danger ahead and avoids it. In the same way that we will never be perfect and sinless wives, our husbands will make mistakes, they will choose wrongly, they will offend and aggravate us. That's just a given considering that we are two sinners trying to live together. The certainty of offense is not a trap we cannot see; rather it is a reality we need to spiritually prepare to face. For all of us, there are things our husbands do that just don't sit well with us. When we make the same choice each time we bump into those areas to respond disrespectfully, we are making the choice to walk into a clearly marked trap. It's as though we see a sign that says, "Road out ahead," and we just keep driving regardless of the consequences.

When we continually fall into those same traps, over and over, we are living the lives of fools. Instead, wisdom would involve preparing our hearts ahead of time to make a good and godly choice by avoiding the trap and continuing to elevate the virtue of respect regardless of the situation of the moment.

We can only live those lives of wisdom as we immerse ourselves in the Word of God and spend time seeking God through prayer. As we are reminded of our own areas of weakness through time in the Word, we will be less willing to dwell on the weaknesses of our husband. As we recognize our own hypocrisy through interacting with the scriptures, we will be less likely to point out his. As we pray consistently and persistently for our husband's growth and wellbeing, we will be more tender and compassionate toward his failings. It's hard to pray for your husband and judge him at the same time!

Ladies, when we choose to fill our hearts with biblical virtues, virtues like: honor, courage, commitment, perseverance, diligence, trust, love, teachability, compassion, patience, self-control, etc., we'll have the strength we need to freely choose to honor God through respecting our husbands. That type of obedience isn't always easy, but YOU CAN DO IT! Remember Master Sergeant Fleger? I highly doubt he "felt" like saluting my husband or any of the other newly commissioned Ensigns for that matter, but he did it anyway. He did it because he so loved the virtue of respect that he was willing to freely choose to humble himself in order to elevate that virtue. It takes faith to live that kind of life. It takes faith to trust that our acts of obedience will bring about godly results. Really, it takes three truths acting in concert to equip us to respond obediently to God. As our *freedom*, (you are free, indeed!) is undergirded by the *virtue* we've carefully cultivated in our hearts, we are then strengthened by our *faith* in the One who calls us and we can do ANYTHING out of a desire to please Him. Believe me, I know it's hard, I know sometimes it's distasteful, I know sometimes our husbands don't deserve it, but I also know this... **You Can Do It**! The God of the Universe is for you and if God is for you, who can be against you?

Way back in the book of Genesis, we are told that woman was created to be a helper for the man. God knew the man needed the woman and more specifically, he knew that *your* man needed you! On the day you said, "I do" you became the only woman that was the perfect fit to complement that man you married. Although different men have a variety of different needs in a wife, every man needs a wife who will respect him. If you will prepare yourself spiritually to respect your husband unconditionally, then you can glorify God abundantly and grow daily in your role as a wise wife.

CHAPTER 3

I ONLY HAVE EYES FOR YOU

"Respect is what we owe; love, what we give."
Philip James Bailey

When you really stop to think about it, in some small way our husbands aren't that different from us after all. The very areas of life where we want to find love are the same areas of life that they're looking for respect. It's actually opposite sides of the very same coin. When our men are feeling respected, it will be so much easier for them to show love to us. And, when they're feeling disrespected? I'm confident we'll know it by their less than loving attitudes. For us, when we're feeling loved, we'll be delighted to show our guys respect. But when we're feeling unloved… look out! That's when we'll be most prone to show our worst side and pull out our: "grouchyanddefinitelynotthewayagirl whosaysshelovesJesusshouldlive" attitude. (If you know what I mean)

Think about how you behave when you're feeling unloved. Are you moody? Depressed? Critical? If that's how we feel, why would we expect our husbands to feel any differently? After 32 years of marriage, I fully expect Steve to know and remember the things that make me feel loved. By the same token, I want him to recall all of the myriad things that make me feel unloved, (like mentioning when I've burned the toast One.More.Time. I swear that toaster is my nemesis!) When he forgets, I'm just as hurt by his forgetfulness as I am by his unloving attitude. It's no surprise that he approaches my respect and disrespect toward him in the same manner. He has made it crystal clear to me over these many years those attitudes and actions that make him feel uplifted and respected and he's also *very* clearly articulated the things I do that tear him down and cause him to feel disrespected. If I expect him to "bump it up" and remember my triggers, shouldn't I assume he'd have the same expectation for me?

The Process of Change

Perhaps, understanding that our husbands are looking for the same thing as us, (just with a different emphasis) will make this process of learning to respect them seem just a little more attainable and a little less intimidating. Really, it's all about changing our focus from a *me-centered* "looking for love attitude" into a *he-centered* "what does he consider respectful" attitude. Sure, changing our focus isn't easy, but it surely isn't impossible. It just takes some hard work. Changing our focus never starts with just changing how we "act" on the outside, though. Instead, it begins with a shake-up of who we "are" on the inside.

Changing our heart attitude doesn't happen overnight, and in fact, it happens in sequential stages. Before we can change our attitude about showing respect to our husbands, we must first understand that showing respect is an actual need. We can come to that realization in a couple of different ways. First, as we spend time in the Word of God seeking to understand how He would have a wife treat her husband, we'll get God's perspective on the whole situation. In a perfect world, knowing that we are doing something that doesn't align with the Word of God and His will for our lives should be all the incentive we need to make permanent and biblical changes in our lives. That's a perfect world though, and unfortunately, not many of us live there!

For most of us, just knowing what God thinks about how we are living and behaving isn't enough to push us to the point of bringing about those necessary changes in our lives. Sadly, sometimes we need to see just how our actions are affecting the man we love. There have been too many times that I could clearly see just how deeply my disrespectful attitude or words had wounded my husband. The hurt was written all over his face! I felt terrible and I would promise him that such actions of disrespect would never happen again; but happen again they did. Why?

You see, just because we have an emotional reaction to our wrongdoings doesn't mean that anything has actually changed. We can mourn, cry, and ask forgiveness for our attitude, but unless we make a decision to radically amputate our disrespectful attitudes the same thing is just going to happen over and over again.

As a young wife, I used to ask God to take away my disrespectful words and actions. I begged him to stop me from showing Steve disrespect and to help me be respectful. Even though I prayed

Just because we have an emotional reaction to our wrongdoings doesn't mean that anything has actually changed.

that prayer diligently, I didn't see the hoped for results. Over the years, I've come to understand what was lacking in those immature prayers for change. God certainly wants me to change. He certainly wants me to honor my husband through respectful actions, attitudes, and communication. He certainly wants me to stop hurting Steve and tearing him down. Actually, He wants me to build him up. However, He won't do it for me. Just as I had to learn to *hate* my sin in order to understand the need for a Savior, I've learned that I have to *hate* my disrespect if I'm ever going to be able to abandon it for good.

When I changed my prayers and began to ask God to help me to *hate* my disrespect, He was faithful to answer my prayers. More and more, Steve doesn't even have to point out my disrespectful responses. As soon as they pass my lips the Holy Spirit brings conviction in my heart and I begin to truly mourn my hurtful and damaging words and actions. When that happens, I can be quick to seek forgiveness and restore our relationship to one of mutual respect and love. Learning to follow the Holy Spirit and give Him free reign in my life has finally begun to bring about the permanent changes in my thoughts and actions that I've always truly longed to see, but that I just couldn't manufacture in my own strength.

Realigning Our Pendulums

I can't begin to tell you the difference that type of praying has made in my life. Instead of plunging ahead and saying the first thing that comes to my mind, (often something sarcastic, inappropriate or disrespectful) because of the working of the Holy Spirit I've learned to slow down and carefully consider what I'm about to do or say. I've learned to so hate the feeling of failing and hurting Steve over and over with my lack of respect that I'm almost overly careful to be honoring and respectful in my relationship with him.

Actually, I'm not sure there is such a thing as "overly careful" when it comes to respecting our husbands. Think about it. Have you ever met a woman that caused you to say, "Wow, she's just **too** respectful to her husband! She needs to tone it down a bit." No? Me, either! If we think of our words, actions, and attitudes as a pendulum, what we really want is for our pendulum to be securely hanging straight down. We want it to be well balanced by immersion in the Word of God and obedience to the will of God. For some of us, our attitude pendulum has swung way out to the side. Because of our continual and disrespectful words, actions and attitudes we've gotten completely out of whack and we need to realign the pendulum. Unfortunately, it's virtually impossible to go from out of whack in one direction to totally balanced and in sync. Instead, we almost always need to swing the pendulum way out in the other direction to eventually and over time become the well-balanced and wise wives we desire to be for the good of our husbands and the glory of God. In other words, if you're far out to the left because of disrespect, you need to swing far out to the right and go overboard in the area of respect. The more you practice respectful words, actions, and attitudes the more quickly your pendulum will become balanced and equalized.

Honestly, most of my respect issues all start in one of two places. They either start right between my ears in that undisciplined mind of mine or they start in my heart. My husband might never know what's going on in my mind or heart, but God knows and He's never satisfied with a fake outward respect that isn't matched by a sincere inward honor for my husband. God knows that I can only "put it on" for so long before my yucky inward attitudes will begin to seep out in sarcasm, disrespect, and ultimately rejection. All of the attitudes we'll discuss in this chapter have the potential to build or destroy. When we become women who live our lives under the control of the Holy Spirit and undergirded by the Word of God, we'll use our heart attitudes to uplift and encourage our husbands. But when we allow our hearts to be filled with cultural norms and worldly appetites, soon what seeps out of us will tear down and destroy the man that we claim to love and damage our ability to show God to a watching world.

But What If I'm Just Spiritually Superior?

Isn't it easy to have a "holier than thou attitude" with our husbands? Frankly, we women, as a rule, spend more time in the Word of God and in bible studies. We're always working on memory verses with the kids, reading bible stories to the toddlers, and attempting to train our teens to live biblically. Obviously, with all that exposure to the scriptures we're just a *little* more spiritual than our men. We can't help it... It's just that God and us... well, the two of us... we're tight!

Now I know you would never verbalize what I just wrote, but be honest, haven't thoughts to that effect run through your mind? I mean, after all, when does he have time to be in the Word? He's off to work, and then it's time with the kids, not to mention the honey-do list. I mean it's not his fault... poor man. He just can't help lagging behind me spiritually. In fact, isn't he lucky to have a spiritual wife like me?

Get it? Do you see how easy it is to begin to elevate our own spirituality and always to the detriment of our husbands. All those "spiritual" activities in which we can be involved as women are wonderful, but they were never intended to puff us up and make us proud! When these types of thoughts begin to invade our marriage, spiritual growth becomes a competition between husband and wife. It's a competition that he doesn't even know he's participating in and he always loses!

Disrespect is the natural outpouring of a wife who considers herself to be more spiritually astute than her husband. She will begin to question his decisions and distrust his ability to lead the family. Sometimes, she'll unwittingly begin to diminish the children's respect for their father as she flaunts her "superior" spiritual knowledge. What an incredibly dangerous place to be.

Christian authors certainly haven't helped with this dynamic. As more and more books and articles are published insisting that husbands must fit into each author's particular and often narrow parameters of spiritual leadership, our husbands can't help but fail. As we wives hold them up to the measuring stick of the "virtual husband" we're reading about, our husbands will be unable to avoid falling short of our inflated expectations and they'll find themselves in a constant state of apology for their perceived shortcomings.

Ladies, be careful what you are ingesting! Books that promote a legalistic view of marriage and leadership can turn your heart against your husband. Read carefully and consider whether the content you are reading is consistent with biblical truths. For example, I have read books that advocated that **all** husbands needed to be self-employed and available to lead their family in devotions at least twice a day. Is there anything wrong with living like that? Absolutely not, but there is nowhere in scripture that narrowly defines a husband's role in such a way. In fact, in the Old Testament times, which many of the authors try use as their template, the men were often gone for extended periods of time to provide food, settle new lands, and wage war. It was hardly convenient for them to run home and do a quick family devotion in between battles!

All Those Other Men

If it isn't books that are warping our view of how our husbands should be living and leading, sometimes it's the admiration we hold for another woman's spouse. Don't misunderstand, I'm not talking here about wrong sexual thoughts for another man, but sometimes we observe our friend's husbands from afar and consider them to be so wonderful that our own husband becomes unattractive to us. Remember, you NEVER know what goes on in any one else's home! I learned that lesson the hard way as a pastor's wife. Even when a couple seems as though they have it all together and are living a "super-spiritual" life, all may not be as it appears. Or perhaps they are living exactly as God would have them live, but that doesn't mean their choices or lifestyle are what God has in mind for you and your family.

Don't allow your respect for another woman's husband to affect or diminish your respect for your own husband! That would be the same as your husband loving someone else's wife because they seem more put together and loving than you. Ouch!

It's funny, but being a pastor's wife showed me just how easily women could gravitate toward and attach themselves to a husband that didn't belong to them. I can't even begin to tell you how many women told me that they wished their husbands were *just like mine*. Now, we all know that no one is perfect and Steve would be the first to tell you that he's a work in progress, but I'd just have to smile and say, "Yes, he's a great man!" Quite honestly, sometimes I said it through gritted teeth. Sundays can be one of the most stressful days for a pastor's family and more than once he and I had to slip away to his office and "get right" before the sermon. In fact, I remember one Sunday night that I was so upset with him that I considered visiting another church. I just couldn't do it though... how could I explain to my eight children that we, the pastor's family, were church shopping...

I almost hate to mention this, but it's becoming a rampant problem among Christian women. If you are gushing over a man on the screen or swooning about the handsome character in your latest Christian fiction novel, there's no other way to say this; you're disrespecting your husband! As surely as pornography is unloving and disrespectful to a wife, women's virtual crushes are just as dishonoring to a husband. Women may not be as easily drawn to visual pornographic images, but they are drawn to pornographic relationships as portrayed in movies and between the pages of many romance novels. These "innocent" forms of entertainment will do nothing but draw your heart away from your husband and emphasize his faults and failings. Ladies, there is no way he can compete with a fictional, airbrushed competitor for your heart. Run away from these temptations for the good of your heart and the protection of your marriage!

Our husbands aren't fools. When we are continually pointing out how "So and so just does such a great job leading his family," or "I think her children are so well behaved because her husband is just sooo involved" they know we're sending our honor elsewhere and robbing them of the respect they are due as our husbands. When we're oohing and aahing over book, television, and movie characters we'll ensure the same result. Again, such actions will NEVER change our husbands. We'll just hurt their feelings, wound their hearts, and remind them that we don't respect them!

Let me meddle in one last area while we're on the topic of a straying heart. Ladies, your heart should belong to your husband. From Genesis straight through the New Testament, all of the instructions to husbands and wives stem from the understanding of a "one flesh" relationship. Although we may never actually flirt with another man or consider leaving our husbands for another man, when we allow our thoughts to wander to any relationship other than our marriage relationship we are doing our husbands a grave disservice and we are willingly walking into a danger zone.

When our husbands disappoint us or when we're feeling squeezed in our marriage relationships, it's so easy to run back to the glory days in our mind. You know, back when our tummies were flat, our arms were shapely, and our hair was bouncing and behaving! At those times, it's way too easy to begin to daydream about our past prom dates, our old boyfriends, or that one who never really noticed us but we loved him from afar. Swoon… (Can't you just hear the violin music playing in the background?) There's a real problem with those daydreams and our wandering thoughts. While our husband is right in front of us in the here and now, love handles, bald spots, and snoring included, that daydream is perpetually eighteen, or twenty, or twenty-two, you pick the best year.

When we let our spiritual guard down, even just a little, suddenly we're looking back down the road of our life and wondering how we ended up so far away from where we started.

Side note: For me, it's twenty-two. Heck, if I could go back to looking like I did then I'd throw myself a "me-party" that lasted for a month! What in the world was I complaining about when I was twenty-two? If I knew then just how soft and squishy I'd be now… I'd have relished every tight muscled moment!

Ok, back to the serious stuff. Seriously, how can our mature husbands compete with the "boy" of our daydreams? Besides, if he was so great back then, why aren't you married to him now? Plus, if your daydream boy were still 18 years old, he surely wouldn't want what you've got to offer! As my own 18 year old son would say, "Gross, mom!"

The Internet and social media have made this problem even more pervasive. Once upon a time, all we ladies could do was daydream and wonder (hopefully) if we'd ever bump into that boy we remembered. Now, media sites like Facebook haven't just made it a possibility, they've made it a probability. I remember the first time my old high school boyfriend commented on one of the videos my kids had tagged me in on Facebook. He didn't say anything inappropriate, he just told me I looked great and he hoped I was well.

Do you know what happened? My heart started racing and my hands got all clammy. I clicked on his name and checked out his profile. I sat frozen at the keyboard wondering how to respond and composing a reconnection post in my mind. All of the sudden, I had a rush of those old feelings I'd shared with him. I FELT GUILTY!!

Why did I feel guilty? I hadn't done anything wrong and neither had he. I felt guilty because my heart belongs to Steve and in that moment I was allowing someone else to draw it away from him. I got up from my desk and went and told Steve what had just transpired. He laughed, but it prompted a great conversation about protecting our hearts. I can't tell you what to do, but we made the decision that day to not add our old boyfriends and girlfriends to our friend lists. That may seem overboard, but we are tasked with protecting our marriages and I'm not foolish enough to think that we're above falling.

Here's a perspective for you. When I told my sons about that quick interaction with my ex-boyfriend on Facebook, they went ballistic. They wanted to totally block him so that he couldn't see anything about me and he couldn't get in touch with me. While I was feeling flattered that my old boyfriend thought I still looked great, (thanks man!) they felt violated. Hmmm… just some food for thought.

In an interesting turn of events, the analytical numbers show that less and less young people are using Facebook as their primary source of online social interaction. Do you know why that is? It's because we parents have taken it over! Middle-aged folks are the most active demographic on Facebook and it's become a great place to find old friends and reconnect old relationships. HOWEVER, I wish Facebook came with a warning label.

Warning!!! Reconnecting with old love interests can be detrimental to your present and future relationships!

I have several dear friends, lovely homeschooling moms who truly desire to live for Jesus, who have found themselves heading down the dangerous road of online marital infidelity. That surely wasn't their intent when they innocently stalked an old love interest, but an idea became a thought, which then became a preoccupation and all the sudden they found themselves in a place that was dangerous and destructive. Around here, we call that the "incremental creeps." When we let our spiritual guard down, even just a little, suddenly we're looking back down the road of our life and wondering how we ended up so far away from where we started.

We HAVE to do better ladies! 2 Corinthians 10:5 commands us to take every thought captive and make it obedient to Christ. I can guarantee you that intimate thoughts toward any man besides your own husband are thoughts that are disobedient to Christ. They are destructive, disrespectful, dishonoring, and destroying thoughts and we must get rid of them! Do whatever it takes, no matter how radical your actions may seem to others. If you just can't control your wandering computer mouse, then shut down your social media accounts. Believe it or not, we lived without Facebook for a long time and we did just fine!

Your relationship with your husband is too important to risk damaging it for "old times sake." Protect his heart in exactly the same way you would want him to protect your heart. Stop now and make a firm commitment to God and your husband. Commit yourself to honoring both by protecting your marriage through disciplining your thoughts and staying away from danger!

Ok, I'm going to take a deep breath and get down off of my soapbox. Can you tell just how passionate I am about this topic?

He'd Be Lost Without Me

How do you picture yourself in your mind? Do you think of yourself as a wife and one member of the marriage team, or do you consider yourself to be the "fixer" of the family? If our husbands begin to feel as though we've made it our mission to swoop in and rescue them from all of their bad decisions, I can promise you that they won't feel respected. On any given day, our husbands are going to make lots of decisions. So are we for that matter. Some of those decisions will be spot on! Some will be "bravo, you did a great job deciding!" decisions. Unfortunately, sometimes those decisions don't turn out so well for either of us. When our own personal decisions go wrong we get to quietly deal with them, but what happens if your husband's decisions take a turn for the worse?

Sometimes our husbands make wrong decisions. Sometimes our whole family has to face the consequences of those wrong decisions they've made. However, when we rush in to save the day and prevent the inevitable consequences, we're doing more harm than good. Our husbands know when they've blown it. They're not surprised when a decision goes wrong and the consequences begin to pour in. As men, God's desire for them is that they would own their mistakes and make right what is wrong. As they do that, they can keep their head up and remain respectable. When we take control they lose that respectability.

One of the hardest things I have had to tell women in counseling sessions is to allow their husbands the freedom to fail. Because we are so intertwined as family members, the failure of a husband can't help but affect every member of the family and that is just hard on everyone. However, when a wife steps in and fixes every problem so that there will be no failure, the husband is never forced to grow, mature, and learn to make wise decisions. Allowing the consequences of failure is short-term (usually) pain for eternally long-term gain, but boy oh boy is it hard to do!

Sometimes, we have to be willing to suffer hard things in order for our husbands to grow in their role as leaders. If they are always trying to make sure our lives are stress-free or if they're fearful we'll make their lives miserable if something doesn't work out the way we want it to, they'll never have the freedom to stretch their wings and soar. If they can fully expect us to "make them pay" for wrong decisions, they'll take the easy road and make no decisions at all!

For many years, I struggled with the amount of time Steve had to spend away from home. I'll be transparent here and confess that I was reading MANY of those biblical manhood books and they all emphatically stated that if a man wasn't home for the majority of the day there was no way the children could be kept from rebelling. I fussed, and fretted, and fumed, and nagged Steve about the amount of time he was away from our family. Of course, at the same time I enjoyed a certain lifestyle that his airline job provided for our family. I'm pretty sure if you looked up the definition of double-minded in those days you would have found my picture…

Then, September 11, 2001 occurred. On that date, Steve was scheduled to be the co-pilot on Flight 11, the first plane to hit the World Trade Center. Through a miraculous set of circumstances, God chose to spare his life, but I was forced to deal with the stark reality that I could have lost my husband. Instead of him being gone from home some of the time he could have been gone forever. God really used that horrific day to shake up my thinking. I realized just how big a God I served and I was ashamed to realize how fearfully I had been living. Should Steve have been taken that day would it have been inevitable that my children would rebel? Absolutely not! God is bigger than that and He was big enough to fill the gap when my husband had to be gone working, too.

Soon after the events of September 11th, Steve began to travel around the country sharing the beautiful picture of substitutionary atonement that was evidenced when Tom McGuinness died in his place on 9/11. He was able to challenge audiences to consider what it meant to have someone die in their place. He was able to share with them how Tom died in his place physically, but Jesus had died in his place long before that to secure Steve's place in heaven. What a wonderful door of ministry God had opened for Him. I have to be honest, though. I think Steve was somewhat hesitant to walk through that door of ministry at first. He knew how much I was already worried about his frequent absences from our family and this new opportunity meant even more time away.

One Sunday, I was able to travel with Steve and hear him share his story. Obviously there was no audible voice, but God spoke to my heart that day. He clearly told me that my husband wasn't a tame kitten to keep safely at home. He showed me Steve through His eyes and I saw a bold leader ready and equipped to minister to others and share the gospel. I don't remember much of that church service, but I do remember praying and asking God to help me "set Steve free." That night I told Steve what I had learned and I told him that I was ready for whatever God called him to do. Steve is a man who is completely committed to following the Lord in faithful obedience, and he would have, but how much easier it was for him to do so knowing that I wasn't regretfully trying to hold him back.

When we think we're taking control to help our husbands, what we're really doing is trying to snatch control for God and that's always a bad idea!

When we don our Superwoman cape and swoop in to be the hero, we rob our husbands of their respectability and we end up treating them like children. Your husband is not your child and you should never treat him like one! When we think we're taking control to help our husbands, what we're really doing is trying to snatch control from God and that's always a bad idea! I get it. I totally understand the temptation to fix things. That's how God made us! Whether it's our children, our friends, our neighbors, or the homeless guy we just met on the corner, we women are fixers. The problem comes when our compulsion to fix things emasculates our man and portrays him to the world as a helpless male.

Think about the most popular sitcoms and movies. Do the women in those shows treat the male characters with respect? Or, are they made to look like helpless, hapless, inept and incompetent idiots. I think you know the answer and it isn't pretty! As Christian women who desire to become wise wives, we must not look like the culture around us. So put away your superhero garb and stand beside your husband as his helper. Encourage him and remind him that you're confident that he can handle whatever needs to be done. Build him up with your respect and watch him bloom!

Patience, Patience

In my way of thinking, I Corinthians 13, which is dubbed "the love chapter," could just as easily be renamed "the respect chapter." Every verse of that chapter is applicable to our marriages; however, two verses in particular are helpful when it comes to considering our hearts and how to prepare them to respond respectfully to our husbands. I Corinthians 13:4 reminds us that love is patient, while verse 7 adds that love always hopes. These two attitudes, when prayerfully applied to our hearts will equip us to expect great things in and for our husbands. When we can take that inward heart strengthening and exhibit it outwardly through respectful encouragement, our husbands will find in us an advocate and optimistic cheerleader.

Patience is just downright hard! I was always that kid who just couldn't wait for the good things of life. I snuck downstairs and opened my Christmas gifts while my parents were sleeping; I ruined surprise parties because I couldn't wait for my friends to know what was coming; I consistently ate the corners off of my birthday cake before my mom could frost it. In fact, after my first two babies were born early, I informed my obstetrician that he needed to deliver baby #3 six weeks early. He wouldn't do what I asked and you can imagine my disappointment when she arrived on her due date!

As I told you in the first chapter, I'm just as impatient about growth and change. I want to be more like Jesus and I want to get there in a hurry. Honestly though, I'm willing to cut myself breaks when that just doesn't happen. You know, I have lots of excuses like: I have a new baby or it was a busy conference season or we've had a lot of company. Even though I'm impatient, I'm still gentle with myself. Sadly, I just can't seem to extend that same mercy toward my husband. When I see an area in which I think he needs to change, or even worse, when he shares an area he's trying to change, I just have no patience with his dawdling. Impatience with his motivation to change is probably my biggest impetus for nagging him. As I've talked to other women, I've heard the same thing from them. We all want our husbands to grow and change and we just wish they'd get on with it!

There's a real problem with that kind of attitude, though. When I am so focused on my husband's delayed obedience (as I perceive it) that I resort to nagging and nudging him toward change, the Lord has no way to get his attention. I become such a distraction to his growth that the very thing I want to see happen becomes an impossible and elusive reality. It's at those times, that God has to get me out of the way in order to finally get my husband's attention. My impatience is really just self-righteous pride and it keeps me from communicating and connecting with Steve in a respectful and God-honoring way. Let me assure you, when God has to move me out of the way it's never fun!

His Own Personal Holy Spirit

Living patiently with Steve and always hoping the best for Steve really go hand in hand. It's easy to get caught in the "things will never change" trap, but according to 1 Corinthians we have no right to remain there. God is in the business of change and He is certainly big enough and powerful enough to bring about any change He deems necessary in our husband's lives. Often the problem really lies with us. Either we're impatient because our husbands aren't changing quickly enough or through our words and actions we send a clear message that we don't believe that they are capable of changing.

One of my brothers used to mutter the expression "Typical" whenever he wasn't pleased with a decision that I had made. Although he muttered, he might as well have shouted to the world, "That's Megan, she'll never change!" His scornful expression discouraged me and reminded me that once again I had failed.

I may not mutter that expression around my husband, but sometimes I'm afraid that's the message he's getting from me when I perceive that he isn't changing quickly enough. Again, such an attitude is firmly planted in my own stinky and prideful heart.

Too often, we think we are the ones who can most clearly see the ways that our husband should grow and change. In effect, we become their personal Holy Spirit pointing out areas of weakness "for their own good." Do you see how deeply entrenched the "I can change him," paradigm is for us women?

Just for the record, there's nothing attractive about a woman in a personal Holy Spirit t-shirt. And Superhero capes come with matching tights, which don't look good on anyone! I don't care if your wearing them for your husband or for your kids, it's just not pretty. As Christian women and wise wives, we should want to have our family members drawn to us because of our compassion, kindness, and wise counsel. When we are, in essence, dressed as their personal Holy Spirit, our family won't be drawn to us. Honestly, they'll be repelled. So take off that Holy Spirit t-shirt and throw it away, refuse to don your super hero cape and instead, clothe yourself with the winsome character of Christ!

Even though our intentions may be good when we try to point out how our husbands should grow and change, the problem is this, we don't know how God would have our husbands grow and change. Oftentimes, the very changes I pray would happen are the very areas of Steve's life that God is using to challenge and fine-tune me. Those areas I see as needing to be changed in Steve's life are actually areas in which God wants to grow and change me! There have been times that I've pushed, prodded, and prayed to get Steve to change to be more of the man I thought he should be and those times have *always* ended in disaster. God doesn't need our help ladies! When we are so busy concentrating on how our husbands need to change we won't have the time, energy, and concentration we need to focus on our own responsibilities; responsibilities like growing spiritually in our personal lives, living obediently in our relationship with God, and loving respectfully in our marriages.

Put On Your Own Oxygen Mask First

From our hearts flow our actions. We have to be committed to personal growth and change. We have to be sickened by our own pride and self-righteousness. We have to be careful to focus on our own areas of weakness, rather than holding a magnifying glass of judgment over our husband's lives. We have to be quick to confess when we are trying to take things into our own hands because we don't trust God to work out our circumstances. We have to allow our husbands to fail without treating them like children or swooping in to save the day.

We've got more than enough to work on don't we! Just as the flight attendants on every flight instruct their passengers to "put on your own oxygen mask first," we must take care of our own growth and obedience before we ever judge our husband's. If we'll focus on our own hearts and training them to be obedient to the Lord, we can trust God to take care of our husband's hearts. Then, when our hearts have been taught by the Word, prepared through prayer, and softened by compassion, we'll be ready to loving "put-on" the outward actions of respect and honor. When we do that our whole family will be blessed!

WHAT THE HECK? PART 1

POTTY PROTOCOL AND BATHROOM HUMOR

I was going to save this section of "What the heck?" for later in the book, but why not jump right in? When it comes to the differences between men and women, nothing quite sums it all up as well as potty etiquette and bathroom humor… so here goes!

It's been said (by men) that women have weird bathroom quirks, (i.e. we have to go "potty" together) but I'm here to tell you that we have nothing on the guys. Following are some of the things I recently learned from the males in my home regarding how men should… and shouldn't… use the restroom.

- If the men's room has three or more urinals, the middle urinal MUST remain empty. When asked why this was so important they replied with horror, "You don't want to be THAT guy!"
- Along the same lines, it is never appropriate to use a stall if you only need the urinal. When asked why this was a rule I was informed that you could pretty much assume what kind of guy a man was by if he used the urinals or not. (Of course, he can't stand by another

man at the urinal because then he's THAT guy, he certainly shouldn't look at any other guys, but still he has to use the urinals, but…Never mind!)

- When in the bathroom there is NO talking allowed. Like none. Zip. Zero. In fact, one son claimed he would wait until the bathroom is totally empty before he'll go in, just in order to avoid running into a bathroom talker. Again…THAT guy!
- In conjunction with the no talking rule is the "Oops, I ran out of toilet paper" rule. Should you run out of toilet paper in a men's room, etiquette insists that you never, ever, ever ask for assistance. When I hesitantly asked what men do if they run out of toilet paper I was met with an incredulous stare and told, "We wait until everyone leaves and waddle to the next stall… Obviously!" There's no, "Hey buddy, can you pass me some squares," there's just silent sitting and listening for the door to close and the relative safety of silence. Perhaps that explains what takes my guys so long in the restaurant bathroom!

Oh silly men! They have no idea what they're missing out on. For women, bathroom time is as good as a cocktail party. We get to share all of those conversations we don't want anyone else to hear. There's the camaraderie of side-by-side booths. I've discovered some of the newest shoe fashions by striking up a conversation with the owner of the really cute sandals in the next stall! Besides, it's all for one and one for all in the bathroom. My toilet paper is your toilet paper! Men just don't understand making the most of a social opportunity!

Which naturally brings me to locker rooms. My two teenaged boys had me crying in laughter as they shared their shock at what grown men do in the locker room. Imagine their disgust when they realized that grown men don't wear their towels when they come from the shower! My fourteen year old exclaimed, "And they **could** use their towels; they have them hanging around their necks!" Oh the teenaged angst ridden horror!

Imagine what would happen if one of those hapless boys wandered into the women's locker room. Heck, forget just walking from the shower, a ladies locker room is the epicenter of "Letting it all hang out!" Between ladies walking around in their bras and panties, to comparing stretch marks and varicose veins, there's not much that's a hush-hush secret in the ladies locker room! Those tough guys wouldn't stand a chance.

Although men have such "delicate sensibilities" when it comes to potty protocol, the same cannot be said for their approach to bathroom humor and bodily noises. Take a deep breath because we're going to talk about that funniest (to men anyway) of topics… the fart.

What is it about men and farting? I don't know a single woman who proudly announces her farting history. None of my female friends regale me with stories about "the fart that won the west." Generally speaking, I don't know a single lady who even wants to admit it when she's had a moment of gaseous indiscretion.

Not so with my men! If farting were an Olympic event they'd all rush to compete. (Who won the gold, Mom?) Even my 18-month old grandson gets in on the action. When his 2-year old cousin Kaleigh "toots" she just pretends that nothing happened. Oliver, on the other hand, giggles and rolls his eyes. And then, he tries to make it happen over and over and over again. Hilarious! Or at least he thinks so. Which is why I'm glad he's still in diapers, because sometimes the Farting Matinee has disastrous results!

Me, I'll never admit an indiscretion! In fact, when Steve and I were newlyweds, the first time I had a "slip," I quickly told him not to worry about it because as a woman, I only had "air farts," no smell to speak of… Yeah, I haven't lived that one down yet!

I mean, come on, what is up with men? I have one son-in-law who traps his wife under the covers until she begs for mercy from the stench. Another will crawl to the door and stick his nose under the crack if his wife has an "incident." Really! Don't men know that they're supposed to pretend that Nothing Happened?

Farts aren't the only smelly inspiration for men. Why else would they shove their stinky workout clothes in each other's faces? Why would they hold their feet up and ask, "Does this smell bad?" When one son was a young teenager, I looked down into his baseball dugout and noticed all of the coaches and players with their arms up and their noses turned toward each other. Yep, you guessed it; they were sniffing each other's armpits!

There's no getting around this undeniable truth… Men and women are just different! That simple fact is probably never going to change, so now there's only one thing left to say:

WHAT THE HECK!

CHAPTER 4

OH BE CAREFUL LITTLE MOUTH WHAT YOU SAY

"Perhaps you will forget tomorrow the kind words you say today, but the recipient may cherish them over a lifetime."
Dale Carnegie

Just as important as the thoughts that run through our minds are the words that come out of our mouths! Whether it's what we say, how we say it, when we say it, or to whom we're speaking our words have the power to build or destroy. In our marriages, all of our sweetest actions can be negated by one negative and disrespectful comment. Clearly, preparing our hearts to live in a loving and biblical manner with our husbands is the first step toward controlling our tongues, but there's a whole lot more to consider as we prepare to display God's glory through our speech.

Our words affect our husbands in several ways; what words we say, how we say those words, and who hears the words we're saying. While men possibly don't speak about their wives frequently enough, (no lie, there have been some men that I've known for months and never realized they were married) women tend to speak too freely about their husbands and that freedom of speech is often to the detriment of their husband's reputation.

What Exactly Are You Saying?

In Proverbs 31, we are told that the husband of the Proverbs 31 woman sits confidently at the city gate. In Old Testament times, the city gate was the place where important business was conducted. The elders of the city held distinguished places of honor at the city gate. Have you ever wondered why God included this little tidbit in the biography of the Proverbs 31 woman? I think it's there to teach us an important truth. The Proverbs 31 woman's husband could sit at the gate with no fear of what others had heard about him. His reputation was intact because he was married to a loyal and careful woman who didn't speak poorly of him to others.

You know how it is ladies. Often, all we know of another woman's husband is what she's told us. If what she communicates is negative and we spread that negative report to others, soon a man we've never met will be viewed with caution and distrust simply because of the words of his wife. He's defenseless against an enemy of perception that he doesn't even know exists.

There's a problem that occurs when we freely share about our marital problems. Generally speaking, our friends will sympathize with us and offer their words of encouragement and consolation. However, when we go home and subsequently restore our relationship with our husbands, those friends are left with a negative impression because of the unpleasant things we shared. How many of you take the time to go back and say, "By the way, I over-reacted the other day. My husband was right." In my experience that just doesn't happen! Our words and the impression they leave can damage our husband's reputation permanently. Then, not only will he feel disrespected at home, but he'll also be dealing with disrespect from a community that only knows of him from your negative reports. That's just not fair and a wise wife will be careful to protect her husband's testimony, rather than destroying it in the heat of the moment.

Sometimes, it isn't our friends that we're running to in order to tattle and gossip about our husbands. (That's the appropriate words to define what we're doing. Sorry, ladies!) Sometimes, it's our moms we draw into the issue. I hope you have mothers that refuse to listen to a bad report about your husband. It's so destructive to family relationships when our husbands must wonder what's being said about them to the in-laws. I totally understand that sometimes you need someone to talk to… just don't thoughtlessly make that someone your mom!

Steve and I have talked about this need to occasionally talk through issues with another woman. I wanted to find a way seek input without treating him disrespectfully. Here's what we came up with and hopefully it will be helpful for you, as well. Steve and I talked about the women with whom I had close relationships. We agreed on two women that he

Our words and the impression they leave can damage our husband's reputation permanently.

felt comfortable with me approaching to share issues and seek counsel. Both of these women loved the Lord, knew their bibles, and were just as likely to call me out, as they were to take my side. Problemo solved!

Pay Attention To This!

Let me make an important distinction at this point. I am talking about normal women in normal marriages with normal marital issues! If you are in an abusive relationship, whether physically abusive, emotionally abusive, or sexually abusive: I am NOT saying that you should remain silent about your husband's abuse. Run; don't walk to your pastor's office! Your pastor has been put in place by God to help you find the assistance you need. Don't remain silent out of any false sense of obligation. Abuse is unacceptable and no abuser deserves to have his "testimony" protected!

Watch Your Mouth!

Now, on to the importance of the words we speak directly to our husbands. The most observable manifestation of how our words can affect our marriage relationship is obviously found in exactly what we say, the words and statements that characterize our communication. Hopefully it goes without saying that as followers of Christ, our communication needs to be free of vulgarity. I say hopefully, because more and more the language of our culture is creeping into our conversations. It used to be shocking to hear an adult Christian woman use bad language, but today… not so much. If you have allowed yourself to speak in such a manner, may I encourage you to Just Stop It! If you speak to your husband using language that is fitting for a sailor, you can fully expect to be treated in a way that fits the words you choose! Respect begets respect and coarse or profane language is just plain disrespectful.

Vulgar words aren't the only words that will communicate a negative message to your husband. Do you use critical or condemning words? It's so easy to speak sarcastically. The word sarcasm literally means, "to tear flesh," and that's exactly what we do when we allow sarcasm to permeate our conversation. I think of it as a fishhook that goes in and then can't help but tear the skin on its way back out. Sarcasm doesn't just go away on it's own; it takes a concerted effort and wholehearted commitment to using only positive and uplifting words in order to erase it from our vocabularies. Be careful, sarcasm like disrespect is one of the "pendulum" character issues. If you've swung the pendulum way out to one side because of your sarcastic communication you are going to have to swing it way out the other direction before you become carefully balanced.

So often, we believe our sarcastic communication is somehow funny, or that it makes an unacceptable comment acceptable because of the way it's communicated. The problem is this: there is always a grain of truth, albeit small, in our sarcastic comments. Although our husbands may laugh uncomfortably at our words, those things we say sarcastically aren't really funny to them. Honestly, sometimes it's just horrible how we speak to our husbands and the other members of our family. Things that we would never say to a friend or even just an acquaintance, we allow ourselves the freedom to say to those whom we claim to love the most. Cutting sarcastic comments and wisdom-focused respectful communication cannot co-exist. Either we will achieve one or the other. For me, I want it to be wisdom-focused and respectful communication. How about you?

Where Did That Come From?

The sixth chapter of the book of Luke makes it abundantly clear that what comes out of our mouths is directly related to what is going on in our hearts. If we aren't doing that hard, heart-work to prepare ourselves to live with our husbands in an honorable and respectful way, we can be certain that what comes out of our mouths will too often be dishonoring and disrespectful. So what's it to be? A good treasure that's sweet and uplifting or the fruit of a heart filled with disrespect and discontent?

In my own life, there is a direct correlation between the amount of time I spend in the Word of God and the words that come out of my mouth. When I'm faithfully immersing myself in the scriptures and on a daily basis asking myself the question, "According to what I read today, how can I change to be more like Jesus?" the words that come out of my mouth are much more encouraging and respectful toward Steve. However, when I'm "too busy" for that intimate time with the Lord, well… Everyone just gets a little too much Megan! I wish I was a fountain of wisdom bubbling over with life-changing counsel, but quite frankly, without the inner working of the Holy Spirit in my life, nobody needs what I'm peddling!

As we spend time in the scriptures, it is so helpful to search out the passages and verses that will help us learn how to communicate love to our husbands through our respectful interactions. Your marriage truly is the primary relationship in your life outside of your relationship with the Lord. Since that is true, it stands to reason that if your marriage relationship is strained or damaged, every other relationship in which your find yourself will be affected as well. That alone is reason enough to scour the scriptures in order to learn how to build up, rather than tear down your primary earthly relationship.

Make Him Strong

Allow me to get you started as you begin searching for just what words will communicate most effectively to your husband. There isn't a person alive who doesn't need the strengthening boost of an encouraging word now and then. Our husbands are no exception to this rule. The workday world provides more than enough words of discouragement, so when they come home our husbands should trust that they are coming home to a wife that will stop that flow of discouraging words and replace it with a flood of encouragement.

The word, encourage, simply means, "to put courage into." Ladies, when your husband is feeling drained and discouraged, you can provide encouragement in a way that no one else can provide it for him. Husbands, who know that their wives trust them and think they are capable of doing great things, are able to take on the daily stresses of their world with confidence and self-assurance. You play an incredibly important role in your husband's life!

It's so easy to allow discouragement to color our mood and poison our words. Honestly, at the end of a long day with the eight Scheiblets, sometimes the last thing I wanted to do was spend my time encouraging Steve… I just wanted him to disappear with the kids and give me some peace and quiet! At the same time, he was

Husbands, who know that their wives trust them and think they are capable of doing great things, are able to take on the daily stresses of their world with confidence and self-assurance.

coming home from a day full of decisions and stresses brought on by his job and ministry. Every day I faced a choice. Would I demand that Steve meet my needs or would I put away my own desires in order to bless him? Quite frankly, he was faced with that same question each day. Whom would it be… him or me?

May I remind you one more time, it doesn't matter what decision your husband would make given that situation. This is about you! Your choices… Your attitude… Your desire to respect your husband and honor God… Our husbands will stand to account before God someday and they will answer for how they showed love to us. We, however, will answer for our own behavior and choices. I'm convinced that God won't be impressed when I tell Him that I would have encouraged my husband more if my husband had just gone first.

Spend some time thinking about the areas in which you can encourage your husband. For Steve, when I encourage him about his teaching and writing he is empowered to teach and write even more. Our husbands don't respond to compliments about their physical appearance in the same way that we do. That's one of those areas of difference that separate men and women. It is the rare man who really cares about "looking handsome." Yes, hopefully our husbands want to dress nicely and keep themselves well groomed, but saying, "You're so handsome," won't mean as much to them as hearing, "You're so beautiful," means to us. Instead, our husbands are encouraged and affirmed when we notice their manly qualities. Whether it be recognizing their physical strength or the way they show leadership, for a husband those types of encouragement are much more significant and they will produce beautiful fruit in your relationship.

May I Ask You A Question?

Sometimes, the words that our husbands need to hear from us are words of exhortation. If you and your spouse have established a relationship of mutual trust, and if your husband is confident that you respect him for whom he is, it will be natural for him to turn to you as a trusted partner and counselor. In that role, there will be times that the words you must speak are confrontational or difficult. A carefully laid foundation of loving respect will make even the hardest conversations palatable. If, however, you are characterized by sarcasm, distrust, and disrespect, your husband will disregard even your wisest counsel.

Couples who function together as a team within a framework of mutual love and respect can have such an amazing impact on the world around them! We all have family, friends, and neighbors that just can't get along and they speak to one another in unimaginably hurtful ways. When we bring the beauty of Christ, as evidenced through our loving and respectful communication, into our relationships with them, we will then find ourselves able to minister truth and grace to those hurting couples. How we communicate as a couple is perhaps our strongest testimony of the changing power of a relationship with Jesus Christ… And all because we've learned to speak graciously and respectfully!

Oftentimes, the best way to lovingly bring up a difficult conversation is by asking good questions. When we gently and respectfully ask our husbands to help us understand the decisions they've made or the course they are taking, they can take ownership of their own decision-making process. Asking good questions will defuse any defensiveness that your conversation might cause and it will help both of you focus on the issue at hand, instead of the tone of the communication.

Put Away Your Weapons

A major part of gracious speech isn't necessarily the words we use, but the way we use those words. Although the words we're using may be "technically" acceptable, if our tone or body language is disrespectful it will change the whole meaning of the communication. I grew up in a family of *hissers* and let me tell you, there's nothing quite as unnerving as a hissed command in the ear! But hissing isn't the only poor form of communication... There are mutterers, whisperers, yellers, screechers, screamers, (picture any 3 year old girl!) mumblers, and more.

None of the aforementioned communication styles is effective. So if they're not effective, why do we use them? Honestly... Because sometimes they work! If we hiss an unpleasant statement at our husband and he responds by doing as we wish, we've learned that hissing works. If we scream at our husbands and they scurry to comply, again our poor communication technique has been technically effective. The problem with all of these communication styles is the fact that they disrespect and demean the person with whom we are communicating. We may get the desired results, (at the moment) but we'll do long-term damage to the relationship. When it comes to how you speak to your husband, do you fall into one of these categories? If so, I cannot emphasize strongly enough the damage that such communication is causing in your marriage relationship. The only solution is to seek forgiveness for you unbiblical communication style and dig deeply into the scriptures to discover exactly how to speak in a way that brings honor and glory to God, while affirming the dignity of your spouse.

I can say with all honesty that I'm not a screamer, or a screecher, or a mumbler, or a mutterer. I don't hiss and if I'm even near a hisser I break out in hives. However, I am guilty of utilizing brutally effective trigger words. What, you may ask, is a brutally effective trigger word? A brutally effective trigger word is any word you can use in a disrespectful manner or tone that always successfully puts your spouse in his place. A word that would be innocent in any other context, when used as a brutally effective trigger word is a dangerous and deadly weapon.

For Steve and me, that brutally effective trigger word is the word, "Whatever." For years, I used that word as the ultimate insult-lobbing, battle-starting fight igniter. "Whatever" conveyed this attitude in one economical word: "What you're saying is of no consequence to me. You can just keep talking 'cause I'm not interested in hearing any more. Your lips keep moving but my ears stopped listening!"

"Whatever" empowered me and infuriated Steve! I'm ashamed to admit just how long it has taken me to get that nasty little trigger word under control. Frankly, it wasn't how the word was affecting Steve that finally shamed me enough to change. (Although how it affected him *should* have been more than enough!) It was when my youngest daughter told me that every time I said, "whatever" she felt as though I hated her. Ouch, ouch, ouch!

I don't know what your brutally effective trigger word or phrase is but I have a stinking suspicion that we all have one. Trigger words are dirty fighting and they have no place in the life of a wise wife. If you aren't sure what your brutally effective trigger word is may I make a suggestion? Ask your husband!

You may not even realize what it is that you say to him that consistently communicates disrespect and put-down. Once you know, it's time to get rid of that nasty varmint. Ask God to help you recognize when the word is on the tip of your tongue and then once you know it's there, practice extreme self-control and lock it back in its cage.

Your Actions Are Drowning Out Your Words

How is your non-verbal communication with your spouse? Again, we can say all the right things, but if our non-verbal communication is sending a different message our words will be meaningless. There are lots of disrespectful non-verbal cues out there for us to choose from. There's shoulder shrugging, hair tossing, head drooping, back turning, and oh yes, my personal favorite… eye rolling.

"Hello there. I'm Megan Scheibner and I'm an eye roller." No kidding! I've basically made eye rolling an art form. If you were to look at my wedding pictures you would immediately notice that I was an eyeball-less bride. I went the whole way down the aisle with my eyes rolled all the way back in my head… Just lovely! It didn't get any better at the end of the aisle when my dearly beloved leaned in and said, "Nice lips, Babe!" (Remember my orange lipstick?) Then, my dad stepped on my train as he walked back to his pew and there was an ominous ripping sound. I spend the entire ceremony unobtrusively trying to reach back and see if my panties were hanging out for the entire world to see! I swear, just thinking about my wedding gives me post-traumatic stress…

As you can probably guess, my eye rolling usually evokes the exact same emotion as my brutally effective trigger word. When

Steve and I are having "heated fellowship" (ahem) and I roll my eyes at him, I can virtually guarantee that the skirmish will intensify and if the TSA was there they'd raise our household terror level to RED, or in other words, **severe**! (Actually, I just read that last paragraph to Steve and he informed me that the next time I say "whatever" or roll my eyes at him there's going to be a major smack down! *Oh the effort it took to hold my eyes still…)*

Just as in the case of your brutally effective trigger word, non-verbal nastiness is dirty fighting and it's got to go. You probably don't even need to ask your husband about this one. I'm pretty sure we all know the non-verbal weapons in our arsenal. Although they work, non-verbal armaments will *never* build oneness, they will *never* encourage positive communication, they will *never* make us more endearing, and we can be assured that they will ***always*** dishonor and disrespect our beloved husbands!

Help! I'm Drowning In Your Words

Maybe you don't use profane language. Maybe you have squelched negative and discouraging words. Maybe you're the Queen of uplifting and encouraging communication. But… do you just talk too much? Chatterbox wives are guilty of a subtle yet sneaky form of disrespect. When they can't get to the point, talk endlessly about anything that comes into their heads, or just fill every silence with words, words, and more words, they are, in effective, holding their husbands hostage!

We all love to talk with our spouses. (Gosh, I hope that's true. You do love to talk to your spouse, don't you?) But, when we just talk too much we are forcing them to steward their time poorly. No husband wants to walk away and leave his wife in the middle of a conversation, but if we haven't learned to control the amount of talking we do, we are forcing him into a corner and barricading him there with brick upon brick of continual conversation.

Don't think I'm judging you! We Scheibners are a talkative bunch. In fact, when I was just a little girl and still Megan Pierce, my mom used to tell people that I'd been vaccinated with a phonograph needle. (You do know what a phonographic needle is don't you? Argh… I'm feeling old!) Talking too much is easy and it certainly isn't limited to any certain personality type. I'm an introvert and often, an excess of words is my way of trying to fit in and feel a part of things. I have an extroverted daughter and her verbal gushing just comes from too many ideas trying to get out all at once!

James 1:19 should really be the marching orders of all Christians, but especially those women striving to become wise wives. It says this: "This you know, my beloved brethren. But everyone must be quick to hear, slow to speak and slow to anger." In other words, we ought to be characterized by our commitment to listening, not by our love of speaking.

I have two "life verses" that I cling to for encouragement to live the Christian life. One of them is my long-term life goal and the other I must repeat to myself a hundred times a day. I found this verse soon after I came to know the Lord while I was in a discipleship study with some other young women. When I read it, I recognized it as the continual reminder I needed of God's desire for my speech and communication. So, while all of my friends were writing down sweet verses about God's promises for their future and His reassurances of His never-ending love for them, I wrote this:

Proverbs 10:19
When there are many words, transgression is unavoidable, but he who restrains his lips is wise.

My shortened version goes like this: "Where words are many; sin is not absent!" Isn't that the truth, though! When I talk too much I can virtually guarantee that my mouth is going to get me in trouble. That's especially true when it comes to communicating with Steve. We'll be having a great time together and then I just start talking about every little thought that pops into my cute little head. If I had all pleasant and uplifting thoughts that might be okay, but since it's so easy for me to drift into complaining or critical thoughts, guess what happens. Pretty soon I say something negative, which leads to misunderstanding, which invariably ends us up in a place I never intended to go. Sometimes I just talk too much!

I think for most of us "over-talkers," this preponderance of words really started when we were young girls. Because the adults in our lives thought that everything we said was just *so precious*, (really probably precocious) they didn't train us to restrain our words. Too much talking doesn't just trap our husbands in conversations that are endless and time-consuming, too much talking keeps us from listening and responding effectively.

I have definitely noticed that when I'm in word-gusher mode, I lack the ability to be a good listener. When I'm so intent on getting *my words*, *my thoughts*, and *my opinions* out there to make *my point*, I tend to interrupt or form my thoughts while Steve is still talking. When that's the case, I certainly don't hear the words he's saying and I'm even less likely to hear the heart he's expressing behind those words. I Hate Being Interrupted! If I feel that way, I'm absolutely sure my husband feels that way as well. That alone should be a good enough reason to curb my flow of words.

It would be easy to just lump every character flaw into the "disrespect for husband" category and let it go at that, but honestly, talking too much is a much bigger issue. Over-speaking is just plain inconsiderate. No one likes to be with a person who dominates the conversation or who just can't stop talking. We avoid people like that and find reasons not to spend time together. Understanding that truth, what are our husbands to do if we just talk all of the time? They can't exactly escape us! What a rotten position to put them in. If they tell us we talk too much our feelings will be hurt and if they just let us go… they're trapped!

Ladies, this is an area in which I believe we need to police ourselves. Listen to yourself speaking. Do you have a constant stream of words flowing from your lips? One of my dearest friends calls this type of over-communication, "Verbal Vomit." I know that's a bit graphic, but quite honestly it paints a pretty accurate picture of what we're doing when we just can't stop talking!

Sometimes, the sweetest fellowship we can enjoy with our spouses is time spent in companionable silence. Don't feel as though you need to fill every empty space with words. Perhaps, this is another "pendulum" area in your life and if that's the case, may I encourage you to discipline yourself to be an empathetic listener and quiet observer of other's conversations. If you can successfully learn to listen and observe, when you do speak people will listen because they'll know you have something important to say and they'll trust that a listening heart has tempered what you're saying. Especially in your relationship with your husband, if he can trust you to listen and truly hear, you'll become his partner in the truest sense of the word.

When Silence Isn't Golden

Just a couple more thoughts about how our words affect our relationship with our husbands and then we'll move on to the next chapter. We've discussed the words we use and their potential to bring about positive or negative results. We've talked about non-verbal cues and how they can become weapons of destruction when misused. We've looked at the problem of just plain talking too much. Now, let's look at communication from another angle.

While the words we use are powerful in the realm of marital communication, silence can be just as powerful of an entity. We just talked briefly about the positive side of silence when it is used to build relationship and encourage empathetic listening. However, there's another side to silence. Silence, when used manipulatively against a spouse, can cause permanent damage and broken relationship. Just as words communicate a message, manipulative silence communicates a powerful message, as well. That message is never positive and uplifting and it never honors our spouse. Silence communicates that what our spouse is saying just isn't worth a response. Silence, when directed negatively toward your spouse, communicates that they, as a person, don't deserve your words. Silence can be devastating.

Oftentimes in our joint counseling sessions with married couples, Steve and I would encounter a couple that was completely different in their communication styles. For whatever reason, the norm seemed to be couples in which the husband was the one who would *let it rip* when there was marital conflict. Both he and his wife would freely tell us about the husband's angry outbursts and gushing anger. There he would sit at the counseling table, ashamed of his behavior and sure that the entire fault in the relationship belonged to him.

So often, the wives of these men would sit silently across the table. In fact, the husbands would tell us that their wives were always silent; they just didn't respond when their husbands were upset or when they were having a difficult conversation. Because the wives never argued or raised their voices, these women often felt as though they were somehow not to blame for the issues in the marriage. That couldn't have been further from the truth.

The spouses who raise their voices or whom become openly argumentative naturally draw all of the negative attention. However, the spouses who sit silently, refusing to engage and communicate, are just as culpable in marital issues. Silence is not an acceptable form of communication when it is used to win the argument or make the other member of the marriage feel as though they are to blame for every issue because of their outward anger. Some of the angriest women I have ever known have been self-righteously silent spouses.

Ephesians 4:15 emphatically tells us that we are to speak the truth in love. In order for that to happen, we must first **speak**! Obviously, our words must be characterized by love, respect, and self-control but we must use our words! The old saying, "Sticks and stones can break my bones, but words can never hurt me," just isn't true; words can breakdown and tear apart a marriage. But equally, if not more devastatingly, silence can wound and demoralize our spouses, while all the while presenting itself as noble and self-righteous. Don't do it, ladies. Don't allow silence to become your weapon of choice. Speak, speak lovingly, speak respectfully, and trust God to use your wisely spoken words as only He can do.

CHAPTER 5

LIFE IS SO UNNERVING FOR A SERVANT WHO'S NOT SERVING

"One act of obedience is better than one hundred sermons."
Dietrich Bonhoeffer

Abraham Lincoln, among others, coined the phrase, "Actions speak louder than words." Although I'm not sure that's completely accurate, it is true that the actions we do and do not carry out in our marriages convey a strong message to our spouses. In the book of I Peter, husbands are instructed to live with their wives in an understanding way. I tell Steve that means he needs to understand all my little quirks, phobias, and just basic weirdnesses! Wives, however, are told in the book of Proverbs that if they want to be wise, they will *build their homes*. I'm certain Proverbs 14:1 isn't talking about the actual manual labor of building a house, but it is talking about the need to be proactive as we pour into our husbands and families in order to build a home that is an accurate representation of Christ in action.

So much goes into building a Christ-like marriage. Whether it's how we speak, how we serve, or how we prioritize our family relationships, the wise wife doesn't do anything haphazardly or by accident. Rather, she prayerfully plans how to make the most of her days in order to bring glory to God. And, a big part of making a successful plan is planning exactly how we will keep our family relationships in their proper order.

Priority Living

According to the book of Genesis, the marriage relationship is the permanent relationship in the home. Someday, those precious, yet time-consuming children will pack up, leave our homes, and hopefully, begin their own "leave and cleave" relationships. I hope that's what you want! Child #6 just moved into her first apartment, and although once upon a time I couldn't imagine any of my children growing up and moving out, I've reached a stage where I'm very much looking forward to it once again being just Steve and me.

If the marriage relationship is our permanent earthly relationship, then it's reasonable to conclude that it should be our priority earthly relationship, as well. Children, by their very nature, will demand our attention. They are smaller, and needier, and (depending on the time of day) cuter than our spouses. If we aren't careful, they will thrust themselves into position Numero Uno and demand all of our focus and care. Basically, those sweet little humans we produced are capable of sucking all of the oxygen out of the room and leaving us with nothing available to give our spouses.

It's just as important for the well being of your children as it is for the well being of your husband that you keep your priorities in order. When your children observe you purposefully respecting their father and making sure that he holds a proper position of honor in the family, they will feel secure and confident. Secure children are successful children and although it would seem that a child-centered focus would ensure that security such is just not the case. Children, who know that mommy loves daddy and daddy loves mommy, have the family-centered confidence they need to take on their world. So, don't feel bad about making your husband your priority! Your kids may fight to hold onto the preeminent position in your home, but if you love them you'll remind them that in your heart and actions, "Daddy is #1."

We can know in our hearts that our husband is our priority relationship. We can even verbalize that commitment to him. However, if we don't take practical steps to firmly place him in that position of priority on a daily basis, our words will be hollow. Following are some practical ways to remind your husband, your kids, and yourself that honoring your husband is your most important ministry.

How do you respond to your husband when he leaves your home in the morning or comes home in the evening? Do you greet him? Or, is he on his own wandering the house looking for someone (anyone) who's glad to see him. I didn't grow up in an emotionally demonstrative family, (Trust me, that's an understatement) and I never saw respect for my father modeled by my mom. When my dad came home from work she never greeted him. In fact, if she looked up from the television to acknowledge him it was only to tell him he was late. With no example to follow, I just didn't know what to do when Steve came home from work. When we were newlyweds and he was still in flight training. I would sit in the bedroom looking out the window in order to see him driving down our road. (To be honest, praying he hadn't crashed and wondering where we kept the insurance papers! No one ever accused me of *under*-thinking...) His flight schedule was erratic and dependent on the weather, so I never really knew when to expect him. Once I saw him coming, you would assume that I went and prepared to greet him, right? You'd be wrong. When I saw him coming I'd get so nervous and awkward that I always found a way to be too busy so that I had an excuse not to meet him at the door.

To this day, I don't know what caused my strange reaction. What I do know is this: By turning my back to work at the stove or going outside to hang up laundry, I sent a message to Steve that I never intended to deliver. Every night, when he came home, he assumed that I was bothered by his homecoming. He thought I wasn't happy to see him and then assumed that meant I didn't love him. Wow! What a lousy message I was sending.

When Steve told me how he felt, I could immediately understand how he'd come to that conclusion and I worked hard to change my actions. Unfortunately, damage had already been done and I found myself as a newlywed trying to dig out of a hole of poor communication that I caused all on my own.

Do you want your husband to know that he's your priority? Greet him happily when he comes home! It's so simple, yet so easy to miss. If our best friend or our neighbor came through the door, I guarantee we'd jump up to greet them. Why won't we do the same with our husbands?

When our husbands know without a doubt that they are our most important priority, they will feel not only respected, but loved as well. When you have the opportunity to go out and do something fun for an evening, with whom do you spend that time? For me, the honest answer to that question is this: It depends.

Sometimes I go out with my girlfriends, but quite frankly, most of the time I go out with Steve. He's not just my top priority; he's my best friend, too! Occasionally, even after I've already made the decision to go out with the girls, I'll cancel my "girlfriend plan" just to spend more time with Steve. My girlfriends and I have all given one another the latitude to make those last minute decisions. They are cheerleaders for my marriage and it's my privilege to cheer for them, too! For Steve, that decision to "pick him" means the world to his heart. It doesn't matter how much time we spend together, when he knows that I am purposefully *choosing* to set aside time for us he feels honored.

Is That Your Boyfriend?

Speaking of spending time together… When is the last time you went out on a date with your husband? When is the last time you were just his girlfriend? Somewhere along the way too many of us grew up, got serious, and lost that "girl" that our husbands fell in love with way back when. The wise wife is a wife who resurrects his sweetheart now and then. It's far too easy for both husband and wife to get so caught up in the daily mundane routine of life and to lose the wonder of their love relationship. If you want your

It's far too easy for both husband and wife to get so caught up in the daily mundane routine of life and to lose the wonder of their love relationship.

husband to know he's your priority make sure he knows that he's your favorite date!

Just a quick side note: May I encourage you to make sure your date lasts for at least three hours. For most women, the first hour and a half is spent wondering what's happening at home. "Did the babysitter make sure everyone ate? Did she burn the house down while she was cooking dinner? Is everyone bathed? Did anyone drown?" You know, all the normal mom worries we carry around every day. After we've worked through the mom checklist (that's about 1.5 hours) we're finally free to stop being mom and become our husband's wife and girlfriend. That's when the fun stuff starts!

Just because you're married doesn't mean you need to stop being playful! Hold hands and slip him little love notes. Text him just to say that you're missing him. Dance in the restaurant lobby, or in the kitchen, or while you're waiting in line at the grocery story. Plan a picnic or take a long walk. Don't let life be nothing but seriousness and bills and doctor's visits and work! Whatever you do, don't allow your marriage to become simply two parents and roommates living in the same home. If that happens, when your children leave to start their own families you and your husband may very well look at each other and realize that you don't even recognize who you've become. More frighteningly, you may realize that you just don't really like each other anymore. Don't let this happen to you! Let your husband know how important he is to you by investing in your marriage each and every day!

When Steve and I teach marriage conferences, we make it a point to encourage couples to find and incorporate some time to get away alone together in order to invest in their marriage relationship. Even just a couple of days away can make a huge difference in the quality of your marriage. We all need times when daddy is just hubby and mommy is just a wife. All of the couples at the conferences nod in agreement when we say they need to get away. I believe they all leave with great intentions of making it work. However, far too few couples ever get to the point of making that special time happen. Why is that?

When we ask the couples what happened and what kept them from getting away together, we almost always get the same exact response. The husband looks at the wife, who looks away sheepishly and says, "It was just too complicated to leave the children, so we didn't go." Argh! Ladies, let me say this again! If you want your husband to feel loved, honored, important, and like he's your priority… make time with him the number one most important agenda of your week! Obviously, there will be times of sick children, overtime work hours, messy finances, etc., but make those times the exception! As much as it is in your power, be that wise woman who builds her home by keeping her husband in his priority position. You do that when you work hard to overcome the obstacles and logistical problems inherent in going away. Trust me, you won't ever regret the one-on-one time you invest in your marriage. You may, however, live to regret the times you said "No" to a marital focus.

Yes, It's Time For The Sex Talk…

Moving along in the same direction… If you want your husband to feel important, honored, respected, and loved you need to make sure he feels desired. That's right… here comes the sex part! I'm speaking as both a wife and counselor now: Nothing makes a man feel more disrespected than a wife that is uninterested in or even hostile toward his sexual advances. If you want to demoralize and destroy your husband just be the wife who is always spring-loaded to say, "No."

I totally understand how tired you are at the end of the day! Remember, I have eight kids and keeping up with them is exhausting. However, I also know how important the sexual component of our relationship to our husband is when it comes to the long-term health of our marriages. Keeping your husband and your sexual relationship with your husband as a primary priority will bear fruit in so many other areas of your marriage.

In our counseling, Steve and I have been shocked at just how infrequently many young couples are having sex. What's up with that, ladies? Sex isn't just a necessary evil that you put up with as a good and obedient wife. Sex is ordained and mandated by God. Trust me, He's never asked us to do anything that He doesn't know is exactly the right thing for us! Besides that, according to the Song of Solomon, God even wants us to have fun while we're following Him in faithful obedience. How awesome it that!

Another sad revelation from our counseling is just how many men have the distinct impression that the only time their wives are interested in sex is when they are hoping for a baby. Whether true or not, that is the impression they've formed because of their wives' behavior and it is causing great harm to marriage relationships.

Although part of our husband's role is to be the initiator in all areas of the marriage, a wise wife will sometimes initiate times of sexual intimacy with her husband. When you initiate sex with your husband you are sending him a message that you are just as interested in him as he is in you! For those who desire to be wise wives and build their homes as found in the Proverbs, the health of the physical relationship is of paramount importance!

What if you've gotten into the habit of saying no? How do we dig our way out of a hole that we have inadvertently dug through fatigue, busyness, or miscommunication? First of all, I would encourage you to have a candid conversation with your husband about your sexual relationship. Ask him to speak truthfully with you and tell you how he's feeling about your level of intimacy. You may be surprised by what he has to say. Make it clear to him that you love him and desire to show him that love through your physical relationship. Then ladies, make it happen! It may mean that you need to nap while the children are napping in order to save your energy for your husband. Or, perhaps both of you need to put those munchkins down to bed earlier so that you aren't both exhausted when it's time to head to bed together. Whatever **it** is that is derailing your sexual intimacy… Get rid of it!

If there are things that make sex awkward or uncomfortable for you, be the one to take the initiative and bring those issues up in conversation with your husband. In one of our homes, an old farmhouse with no lock on the bedroom door, I was just so nervous when Steve and I were sharing times of intimacy. How easy it would have been for me to communicate that concern, but instead I just inwardly fretted about my fear that the children would come barging in and be scarred for life. (Sometimes I'm maybe a little overly dramatic) Steve had

Although a healthy sex life isn't all that's key to a healthy marriage, it's certainly one of the cornerstones.

no idea what was wrong; he just knew something was going on and I surely wasn't relaxed. After about the tenth time he asked me what was bothering me, I finally told him. (Why ten times? Who knows… that's another one of those poor and manipulative communication techniques we employ) The very next day he bought a lock and installed it on the door. Problem solved… which it could have been weeks earlier if I'd just spoken up! In another house, we had an older daughter occupying the room next to ours. I realized that if I could hear her singing along to her radio she could her us______ (I'll let you fill in the blank) The next day we initiated a room swap and moved the nursery next to our room. (So that I could be closer to the baby, of course. That's my story and I'm sticking to it!)

Although a healthy sex life isn't all that's key to a healthy marriage, it's certainly one of the cornerstones. Do you want your husband to know he's loved and respected? Then make sure he knows he's desired and appreciated!

For years, Steve and I included a "sex talk" in our Marriage Matters weekends. To be honest, we had to drop the talk because our audiences would get so silly that we'd have to take a "composure break" in order for everyone to get it all back together. In our talk, we referenced a book entitled, Men Are Like Waffles, Women Are Like Spaghetti. (Great title, so-so book)

In the book, the author stated that generally speaking, men live their lives in little blocks… like a waffle square. They have the getting dressed square, and the work square, and the now I'm playing with the kids square, and of course, the sex square. For men, everything is compartmentalized and they usually choose to focus on one area of their life to the exclusion of all other areas.

Steve's explanation is even easier to understand. He says that men are like a light switch. They're either off or on, and they can go from off to on pretty darn quickly.

Women, according to Men Are Like Waffles, Women Are Like Spaghetti, are more like a noodle. Unlike men who live their lives in little boxes, women live lives of connection. For them, everything is intertwined and connected on the noodle of their life. I call it the "Love Noodle," because basically, all of the connections send one of two messages to a woman. Either we hear, "I love you," through our daily interactions with our husbands, or we hear "I don't love you." When the message is "I love you," all is well. However, regardless of how the rest of the day has gone, if one little incident conveys the "I don't love you" message, the noodle is broken and a woman tends to shut down emotionally. And obviously, if she's going to shut down emotionally, she's going to shut down physically as well…

Steve also simplified this explanation. He says that women are like irons. You know how it works… First a man has to find the iron. Then, he has to plug it in. Then he has to set it on Linen, (the hottest setting by the way) and then he has to wait for it to warm up. Of course, while he's waiting he has to check it now and again, just to see how hot it's getting, and then finally, when it's super hot and ready to go… Good things happen! Husbands can get their own personal "irons" ready as they practice little acts of kindness and service throughout the day and as all those little actions connect on their woman's love noodle.

Let's go back to that noodle illustration again. While the illustration seems to make complete sense, (to women, anyway) there's a problem with living like a noodle. Say a husband sees a delicious bowl of spaghetti in front of him, spaghetti that is full of pasta and heaped over the side of the bowl. (No, that's not a fat joke!) But what if upon further inspection of that bowl of spaghetti, he realizes that there's only ONE noodle. One long, stretched-out-forever noodle. How in the world would he ever enjoy that delicious bowl of spaghetti? He'd be winding and winding and winding, but the noodle would never end.

Ladies, sometimes we're like that bowl of spaghetti. Our "love noodles" can be so long and stretched out that regardless of how many kind acts our husbands perform, how many sweet words of encouragement they share, how many different way they serve us... they still can't ever get to the end of that darn noodle! When that's the case, eventually they're going to get tired of trying and just give up and go eat a bowl of cereal!

If you think there is even a remote possibility that you've been living the life of a super-long love noodle may I offer some "kick in the pants" encouragement? Perhaps, you need to live more like elbow macaroni. Or, possibly you could be an Acini di Pepe. (Not sure what that is? Look it up! But I'll give you a hint: it's a teeny-tiny pasta shape.) Or maybe, just maybe, you should simply be alphabet noodles and spell out the word, YES!

So to sum up the always awkward, but certainly necessary section on sex:

You have what your man wants and he has what you need so you should tell him that you want what he has and that you're excited to give him what he needs and then you two go do what you do and be blessed... 'Cause God says its ALL-GOOD!!

Whew! Aren't you glad that's over?

I Heard That Guy Thinks You're Cute!

Are you ready for another, "What! He thinks that's disrespectful?" area of marital miscommunication?" This one took me a long time (and many disagreements) to understand, but now as I'm watching the same dynamic play out in the lives of my married kids, I'm finally getting it.

How do you respond when your husband pays you a compliment? Do you graciously thank him or do you ignore the compliment, respond nervously, or worst of all... disagree with him? I can't even remember how many times Steve has complimented me and I've responded in any number of ungracious and unthankful ways. I certainly didn't think I was being disrespectful at the time, but to him, the giver of the compliment, my ungracious replies were basically the same as accusing him of lying.

When our husbands compliment us and we respond poorly, they don't see that response as humble, or embarrassed, or meek, or any other positive character quality. They see our response as an argument; a negating of what they see to be true.

Let me share a secret with you ladies. I know for a fact, that when you look at your reflection in the mirror and when your husband looks at you, the two of you are NOT seeing the same woman. We women look in the mirror and see double chins, dark circles under our eyes, jiggly bellies, and back boobs. (Why God? Just Why?) Your husband, on the other hand, sees some variation of this: "Wow! That's my woman! I like my woman! I wonder what my woman is doing later on tonight!" (More or less)

Seriously, you are beautiful in his eyes! If we could just grasp that concept and hold on to it for all it's worth, what a difference it would make in our daily lives and level of self-confidence. Do you get it? Your husband… the only man who really matters… thinks you're "all that!"

When we refuse to accept our husband's evaluation of our beauty and worth, we hurt their feelings; we make them feel disrespected and unloved. I suppose if there's anything that could make us unlovely in their eyes, that type of response is the thing that could do it. I know it's hard to accept a compliment when you have spit-up in your hair, rice cereal on your shirt, and you're still wearing the same yoga pants that you slept in last night, but you can do it! I know it seems ludicrous to imagine that you're anything more than the mini-van chauffer and an underpaid laundry lady, but to him, you are! I know it seems like a joke to hear that you're so sexy when you're hair is turning grey and the only dimples you still have are on your knees, but he means it!

Practice in the mirror if you must, but for heaven's sake, learn to accept his compliments with grace and dignity. Here, say it with me, "Thank you, that means so much to me!" When you remember that his compliments come from a heart that finds you just as exciting and desirable as you were on the day of your wedding, it will get easier and easier to mean what you're saying and to accept his compliments with joy! Actions come before belief sometimes and if this is one of those times for you, then practice, practice, practice!

Time To Get Busy

Ok, just two more areas to discuss regarding how we can respect our husbands through how we live with them on a daily basis, and then we'll get on to the next topic. This next area is a "doing" area and I'll be honest, "doing" areas are so much easier for me. If I could just get away with "doing" and not have to worry about the "being" and that whole "thought life" thing… Life would just be so much easier. But guess what? God cares just as much if not more about how I'm being and thinking as He does about what I'm doing. That's why it's taken so long to get to this next topic: Serving our own husbands in a way that is meaningful to them.

Please notice that I said "our own" husbands. Oh my goodness has there ever been a lot of bad teaching on this subject! When I was a new bride, every book I read added to the "to do" list of things that were the most important for every bride to do in order to serve her husband. Trust me, if I'd done everything in those books I would have put the Proverbs 31 woman to shame! I'm still not sure how I could have gotten up before him to tend to the obligatory chickens, cooked, cleaned, worked 9 to 5, had well-trained and spotlessly clean children, and still managed to meet him at the door in a "sexy little number!"

Let me set the record straight on this one once and for all! God gave you that husband of yours. He also gave you to him! (Isn't he a lucky guy!) In the same way that you are not like any other wife on this planet, neither is your guy like any other husband. That's why the "to-do" lists just don't work. Trust me, if they did I'd come up with a gloriously organized and color-coded list for you to work from. I'd encourage you to live by the list and die by the list. I'd even tell you to add things that you'd already done, but that you'd

A wise wife is a full-time student when it comes to majoring on her husband.

forgotten to write down, to the list just to cross them off and feel better about yourself. I'd LOVE to give you a fail proof list! But I can't. I just can't!

Your husband is different, and special, and unique just the way God made him. The beauty inherent in serving each of our husbands in a loving and respectful way is that we get to *study* them. We have the privilege and responsibility to really get to know them and to understand their likes, dislikes, quirks and oddities. A wise wife is a full-time student when it comes to majoring on her husband. You aren't called to serve some generic man, but you are called to serve your specific man.

My Steve is different than any other man I have ever known. He's an incredibly hard worker and an off-the-scale idea guy. What that has meant in our marriage is that he is always up to something. When we were newlyweds that meant flying for the Navy and volunteering with Young Life. Next it was working for American Airlines and serving in the Naval Reserves. Soon after came working for American Airlines, serving in the Naval Reserves, and going to seminary to receive two Master's degrees. That busyness was followed by working for American Airlines, serving in the Naval reserves, working toward his Doctorate, and planting a church in Maine. As if that wasn't enough, while doing the above, he added training and becoming a Federal Flight Deck Officer. (In other words, an armed airline pilot)

Things have finally begun to slow down. Now he only works for American Airlines and is the president of our non-profit ministry, Characterhealth, which puts him on the road speaking and teaching around the country. All that to say this: Serving my husband probably looks nothing like what you would do to serve your husband! That's ok! I'm absolutely convinced that God knew exactly what He was doing when he brought our lives together. He knew exactly what He was doing when He put your husband and you together, too. Even when His plan doesn't seem so obvious it's the perfect plan!

When we were engaged, people used to ask Steve what he first found attractive in me. His answer was always the same. He told people that he had been impressed by just how capable I was. CAPABLE! Are you kidding me? I was hoping for pretty, or sexy, or even just sweet... It isn't that Steve doesn't think that I'm those other things; it was just that even back then, he had a sense of what his life would be like and he had diligently prayed for a wife that would be able to handle the daily stress of his craziness.

Serving Steve means making sure that when he is home, he comes home to a sanctuary, a safe haven of peace and order. Steve grew up in a broken home with a drunken father and an even harsher alcoholic stepfather. He was a latchkey kid from the time he was five years old and he'd never known what it meant to be cared for and treated as any type of priority. Clean spaces and an orderly home make him feel relaxed and undistracted.

Remember the big newlywed breakfast battles? Steve's whole life he had dreamed of having a wife who would fix him breakfast. As a little boy headed out the door to school with nothing to eat, his greatest wish had been for a warm breakfast and loving send-off to start his day. He'd never been the kind of guy that shared all of the personal hurts from his childhood, although I knew it hadn't been an easy one. Instead of baring his soul, he just made a simple request. He asked me to make him breakfast and as you already know... I said no!

Is there something your husband wants, something that would bring him joy that you are just refusing to provide for him? I'm not talking about anything immoral or unlawful, I'm just talking about the common, daily, run-of-the-mill requests our husbands make of us. I'm convinced that most of the time it isn't that we *can't* do what our husband's have asked, it's just that we don't *want* to do it. Whether it's our inherent laziness, or forgetfulness, or simply an attitude of "who does he think he is?" we withhold good when it's in our power to give it.

James 4:17, says this: Therefore, to one who knows the right thing to do and does not do it, to him it is sin. Again, in Proverbs 3:27, we are instructed: Do not withhold good from those to whom it is due, when it is in your power to do it. I'm afraid we waste our time finding umpteen reasons why our husbands don't fit into the "to those whom it is due" category. Why in the world would we miss a chance to bless the man we claim to love? May I be vulnerable with you? I completely knew that I should get my sorry rear end out of bed and make my husband breakfast. I just didn't feel like it. I chose a road of argument and distance, rather than blessing and oneness. According to the book of James, I chose the path of sin. I can't begin to tell you how thankful I am that God didn't let up the pressure! It was a lesson I needed to learn and I'm glad I learned it early in our marriage!

Do you realize just how greatly God is aching to bless your obedience? The breakfast fiasco was just the beginning of me realizing this truth. You see, once I finally submitted to God, (that's really where the battle originated) and began to make Steve breakfast before he left for his flight training, I went all out. I was ashamed of my lousy behavior and attitude and I wanted to make it up to Steve. He'd never seen breakfasts like I began to prepare for him. I'd make bacon and pancakes dotted with fresh fruit. I made fancy oatmeal with all kinds of toppings. He had French toast, eggs any way he liked, and breakfast burritos. The man was eating like a king and I was loving (finally) the opportunity to serve him.

My guilt was gone, he was grateful, and I was seeing the blessing of obedience to God carried out in my marriage. But remember, as we learned in an earlier chapter, our marriage isn't ever just about us, and God was about to show me that truth in action.

When we checked into our first active duty squadron after flight training, Steve was assigned to a flight crew. That crew flew every mission together and they habitually drove into work together. Flying for the Navy was never a nine to five job. In fact, each crew flew a certain amount of hours on a mission, then they would rest for twelve hours, then off they went to fly another mission, just to come back and rest for twelve hours, and on and on it went.

This crazy schedule meant that sometimes Steve's flights would be scheduled in the middle of the night. After sleeping all evening, he would have to get up, get dressed, and wait for the crew to pick him up. Those late nights became the start of his day, so guess what I faithfully did each time he had a late night flight. Yep, you guessed it! I got up and made him one of my extravagant breakfasts. Then, I'd pack him a lunch, slip in a little note, and kiss him goodbye at the door.

A Silent Testimony

Something began to happen when the members of his crew observed what was happening. First, they asked him why all of the lights were on in the house. When Steve told them I got up and made him breakfast before he left, they were flabbergasted. Their wives, generally speaking, told them not to turn any lights on because they didn't want to be awoken when their husbands left.

Then, the guys began to see Steve pulling out his carefully packed lunches and reading the little love notes that I had included for him. The guys on the crew were eating boxed lunches from the squadron mess hall and Steve was eating homemade cookies and other special treats.

Word spread and pretty soon, I had wives calling me to let me know that just wasn't how it was done. I was spoiling Steve and it needed to stop. They didn't appreciate the grief they were getting from their husbands and they just thought I was kind of "over the top." I could have just laughed when they called or just gone along with what they were saying, however, it was obvious to me that God was opening a door of opportunity. For years, Steve and I were the only Christians in that squadron and I prayed consistently for open doors to share about a relationship with Christ. Those early morning breakfasts pushed the doors wide open.

Every time I received a call from one of the other wives, or when one of them would corner me at the wives club meetings to tell me to "knock it off," I told them the whole story. I talked about my stubborn heart and willful pride. I told them that it was that very pride that Jesus had died for on the cross. I used the lesson that God had brought into my life to testify of Him. Through those talks, I was able to start a bible study with several of the wives from our squadron. Making breakfast for Steve became a catalyst for change in families with whom both Steve and I were now able to share biblical truth, and then encourage trusting in Christ for their salvation.

I didn't make breakfast for Steve because I was looking for praise from the other husbands. I didn't assume that making him breakfast would open doors of ministry. I just did it because it was the right thing to do; it was right to serve my husband because he's worthy of my service. It was God who saw the bigger picture and it was God who used pancakes and bacon to bring glory to Himself. I never could have planned for that to happen.

It's been 29 years since we were in that first squadron. Just last year I had the opportunity to be reunited with one of the dear wives with whom I had shared my story. She was one of the ladies who faithfully attended my bible study. Shortly after we all left the squadron for new duty stations, her husband had been killed in a tragic mid-air accident. She was expecting her second child at the time and was left a widow at 26 years old. As we reconnected at the reunion, she shared with me a memory from her husband's funeral. She said, "I remember you kneeling beside me and reading from the bible. You gave me that bible and I've read it every day since the funeral. You gave me something to hold on to and I'm forever grateful."

I've cooked literally thousands of breakfasts since those early newlywed days. Thousands! In fact, chickens around the world shudder when they see me approaching. But I have no desire to be remembered as a great breakfast cook. I want my legacy to be as a woman who pointed to Christ in everything she did. What will your legacy be?

There is always a bigger picture and that bigger picture always points to God.

What Testimony Are You Cooking Up?

Just as a reminder, making breakfast for your husband may NOT be the way that you are called to serve. Remember, every husband is uniquely different! Years ago, one of my dear friends heard me share about how God worked in my heart by convicting me in my heart of the need to get up and cook for Steve. She went home and tried to serve her husband in the same way and it just didn't go so well. In fact, he asked her to stay in bed and let him get his own breakfast. The morning time of peace and quiet was important to him as he began his day and chatting with his dear wife just didn't fit his needs. Trust me, she found other ways to serve her husband and she is an excellent testimony of a wise wife with a blessed marriage. It isn't about just serving… It's about serving in a way that is distinctively suited to your husband.

Ladies, your service to your husband may very well be the specific vehicle God has chosen for use in your life in order to meet the exact needs of the ladies watching you; watching to see how a woman who claims to love Jesus actually lives. There is always a bigger picture and that bigger picture always points to God!

There are lots of other ways that I serve Steve, and quite frankly, some of them have meant discarding old habits and learning new and sometimes uncomfortable ways of serving. I grew up in a terribly messy home. My mom would probably have been defined as a hoarder, so I certainly hadn't been trained to keep a clean and orderly home. To serve Steve well, I had to change old habits and establish new routines in order to make our home a peaceful sanctuary and a place of restful calm to counteract his busy life. Through learning to serve Steve in this way our whole family has been blessed and I'm delighted now as I watch my own daughters serve their husbands by how they run their homes.

Matching His And Her Responsibilities And A Simple Economic Principle

I came into marriage with quite a long list of things that I was certain were "man jobs." I'd seen my dad carry out certain jobs in my home growing up and so I just assumed my new husband would take on those jobs as well.

Just a quick side note: Don't assume anything! Assumptions and expectations cause nothing but strife. If you're thinking it... communicate it! The final answer may not be what you want to hear, but by not communicating what you're hoping to see come about, you're just setting yourself and your husband up for failure.

Speaking of assumptions and expectations... Be careful of the cultural mindset that declares your marriage a 50/50 proposition. Such thinking isn't biblical and it will cause seeds of bitterness to be planted deeply in your heart. The only harvest you'll reap from those seeds of bitterness is distance, disappointment, and destruction. If marriage truly was a 50/50 proposition, I'm sure I'd find a way to measure my actions and determine when I'd completed my 50% and then I'd sit back and judge Steve's proportion of the marriage. Marriage is actually a 100/100 proposition. Each partner in the marriage relationship is responsible before God to do their 100%. I've found that when I'm focused on performing the 100% that belongs to me, I have little or no time to check on Steve and make sure he's doing his 100%.

Remember Steve's crazy schedule? From the very earliest days of our marriage, that schedule made it obvious that in our lives a separate list of "man jobs" just wasn't going to cut it. If I waited for Steve to come home from his nine-month deployments in order to take the trash out, we'd have been in a big stinky mess. When he was gone on a 9-hour flight and the car died by the side of the road, I couldn't exactly call the flight crew and have them patch me through. "Honey… I have a little problem!"

Even when Steve was home, he was still always busy and his busyness was always either service for the Lord or extra work to help us pay the bills while allowing me to stay home. Every day, I faced a choice. I could set aside certain jobs and leave them for Steve to take care of or I could just take care of them myself. It really came down to a win/lose economic principle. If I left the jobs for Steve to complete, I lost the hours that we would have had available to spend time together as a couple or family. For me, it was always worth doing everything I possibly could to make his "home" work lighter in order to gain precious family time.

I'm actually quite impressed with myself right now! I showed Steve that last paragraph and he pointed out that I just used an economic principle correctly for one of the few times in my life. That's a milestone! You see, when I met Steve in college he was an economics major. I needed one more elective in order to graduate and I chose economics. I took it as a Pass/Fail class and believe it or not, I failed! That was the ONLY class I ever failed. Actually, I failed because I cut class so many times… I just couldn't get past the boredom factor. When it came time for the final exam, Steve was desperately trying to explain the difference between a "smiley" face and a "frowny" face on the graphs to me just so I would pass the class. To think, I could have taken a basket weaving class as my elective... What the heck!

Steve was right; he needed a capable wife. Your husband needs a capable wife too! You capability will look vastly different than mine, but I guarantee that there are areas of service for your husband that will lift the load from his shoulders and speak volumes about your love and concern for him. Don't be content with the status quo. Tell your husband that you want to serve him better and ask the question, "How can I serve you?" We only don't ask because we don't really want to know; knowing requires action! A wise wife wants to know.

Where's The Applause?

If you set out to serve your husband in practical and proactive ways, don't expect all of your friends to applaud and give you kudos. Unfortunately, in many ways a wife who is attentive to her husband's needs is no longer the norm in our society. Don't let snide comments or sarcastic jokes sideline you from following God in faithful obedience. Once you have sought the Lord in prayer, and asked your husband in person, just what service would be the most honoring for you to carry out, proceed with confidence. Allow your good character and your sweet marriage relationship to stand as your testimony. In the same manner, when you see friends trying to honor God by serving their husbands, make it your ambition to encourage them and tell them that you notice their sacrificial acts of love. Surround yourself with women who will encourage your growth and hold you accountable to live out what you say you believe.

A Time To Speak

Finally, a wise wife lives with her husband respectfully and carefully when she considers wisely the right time to discuss difficult topics. This really could have fit into so many of the chapters because it is part of how we speak to our husbands, part of what we're thinking about them when they're not with us, part of being teachable and ready to receive exhortation from them, but for simplicity's sake, let's just address it here.

I believe we fail in our communications and cause strife needlessly when we don't respect our husbands enough to give them space and time when they need it. Most of the women I know want to solve problems now, now, now. Men, on the other hand, need time to process and contemplate, and sometimes, they just need to wind-down before they're prepared to tackle the next big issue.

I get it. We have all day to think about the big "thing" that is on our minds. For us, it makes absolute sense to deal with the issue quickly and emphatically. For our husbands, however, coming through the door from work and being handed a new situation or dilemma to solve is like being ambushed by a waiting tiger. When that happens, they are likely to respond defensively or make hasty and knee jerk reactions. Then when they don't respond the way we think they should, (after all, we've had all day to come up with what *their* correct response should be) we are upset and compound the problem by reacting harshly or disrespectfully.

This problem can be easily avoided. It's just considerate and respectful to give our husbands a few moments to get home, unwind, and prepare to re-enter the home environment. When we practice self-restraint by delaying our need to discuss and fix problems immediately, we allow them the space they need to prepare to switch gears from work to home.

When your husband first comes home from work is a wonderful time to incorporate what Steve and I call "talk time." Invest 15 minutes in your marriage by just talking with your husband about pleasant topics. Don't discuss the naughty children, the broken toilet, the over-due bill, or anything else controversial. Instead, spend time focusing on one another. Don't use talk time as an opportunity to unload all of your concerns on to his waiting shoulders. Trust me, you would want your husband to do the same! On the days that I have occasion to be out of the house and Steve is at home in charge of the kids, I feel especially loved if he gives me a few moments to regroup when I get home, instead of filling me in on all of the "mommy-needs" that are on hold because for some strange reason only I can fill them!

The same basic principle holds true when you and your husband are stuck in one of those circular discussions. When you keep rehashing the same issues over and over, without being able to come to a point of resolution, a wise wife gives her husband time to process. Again, just the simple act of giving our husbands some space will allow them to slow down and think carefully without the defensiveness that comes from a continual barrage of words.

This is one area, in particular, where respect equals self-control. *Can* we push to discuss things immediately and until we've reached a definitive conclusion? Absolutely… we *can*. But, *should* we? Wisdom shows itself through consideration for our spouse; it's a simple "Do unto him as you would have him do unto you," proposition.

A wise woman builds her home. What are you doing to proactively build your home today? Doing nothing is the same as tearing down your home. A marriage that isn't purposefully protected and nurtured will begin to show signs of destruction and decay. Respectfully serve your husband and keep him as the priority relationship in your life. You'll be blessed by the love he gives you in return!

CHAPTER 6

DO YOU REALLY WANT TO CHANGE?

"It's one thing to give out excellent advice, but quite another to personally swallow it."
Richelle E. Goodrich

How do you feel about that pesky Proverbs 31 woman? Love her? Envy her? Hate her and wish you could run her over in the church parking lot? Love her or hate her… God put her in the scriptures for a His own good reasons and those good reasons certainly include our good and His glory!

I've heard so much teaching about the Proverbs 31 woman in my many years of walking with the Lord. Sometimes the teaching was sarcastic and irreverent. Sometimes she was taught as a law and by golly I'd better be living up to that law. Sometimes she was used as a hammer over my head and more times than I can count, she was a Mother's Day sermon meant to make me feel better about myself. Regardless of the occasion, the majority of the time Proverbs 31 was upheld as a holy to-do list and quite frankly, a discouraging glimpse into all of my own failures.

I have some good news for you! We're going to change our perception of that hardworking and much-maligned biblical sister. I want to take our eyes off of the to-list and put them right where they belong… on the heart; and in particular, our heart.

Context Is King

Let me ask you a question. To whom were the Proverbs written? Think about that for a minute and if you need to… go look in your bible. That's right, the Proverbs were written to men and Proverbs 31 is no exception. It's not as though thirty proverbs were addressed to men and then God said, "Oh wait, I'd better give those women something to consider too." Does it seem a little strange to you? Does it seem odd that a list of womanly goals and character qualities would be written to a man? Let's dig apart this section of scripture and hopefully by the time we're done, it will make more sense.

*As we're working through this chapter of the book, it would be helpful to have your bible open next to you in order to cross reference what I'm saying and keep me honest!

The first verse of Proverbs 31 tells us exactly who was doing the teaching and whom was the intended pupil. This proverb was an oracle taught to King Lemuel by his mother. (More about her later) Often, when Proverbs 31 is taught from the pulpit or at a ladies conference, we skip right over verses 2 through 9 in a rush to get to the "good stuff." These verses are so important, however, because they lay the groundwork for what this loving mother was about to teach her son.

Although verse two, on first glance, may just look like a repetition of names by which Lemuel's mother referred to him, it is actually her way of calling attention to what his life as King was going to be all about. As the King, he was going to be called upon over and over to answer the "what" questions of life. "What shall we do about the uprising of the peasants, your Majesty?" "What do you want to do to celebrate the anniversary of the Kingdom, Sire?" "What land shall we conquer next, oh King?" You get the picture. His role, because of his title, was going to involve leading, guiding, and making daily decisions for the good of his people.

After establishing his role, Lemuel's mother then went on to warn him of the things that could rob him of the ability to make the wise decisions he would be called upon to make. In particular, in verses three, four, and five, she warned him of wayward women and drinking liquor to excess. In other words, she told him to avoid "those women" because they would distract him and cause destruction in his life. She cautioned him to avoid strong drink; reminding him that in his drunkenness he could be tempted to forget the laws of the land and misuse justice for his own gains.

In verses six and seven she made a point of contrasting his life, with the life of those who need such strong drink; those who are perishing or living lives of bitterness. Hardly the life he would be living as the King. Verses eight and nine then challenge him to use his title to do good in the kingdom and to help the unfortunate and defend the afflicted and needy.

And Most Importantly...

Can't you almost picture Lemuel sitting by his mother's chair as she stroked his cheek and gave him such valuable counsel? After laying out his role, the pitfalls that could keep him from ruling nobly, and the ways he could use his title to full advantage, this wise mother then spent twenty one verse talking to her beloved son about the most important earthly relationship he would ever enter. She counseled him regarding the most significant person he would have in his life… his wife.

She begins her counsel with this simple, but often misunderstood question: "An excellent wife, who can find?" Although the language used here is lovely and poetic, it doesn't help us as we seek to truly understand this proverb, so let's reword that sentence according to the original meaning. Grammatically ordered, the sentence would read: "Who can find an excellent wife?"

Now slow down… before your brain settles on what that sentence means, we need to dig just a little bit deeper. In the original Hebrew language, the word "find" has three possible meanings. In order to correctly understand Proverbs 31:10, we need to understand that word in it's original definition.

The first meaning of "find" implies something that we come upon in a haphazard way. Imagine that you're walking through the mall parking lot and a hundred dollar bill blows right on to your shoe. You pick it up and look around, but there is no one in sight. Jackpot; it's yours! If that were me, I'd shove it in my pocket and head to the nearest boot store! You call your husband and say, "Guess what! I **found** a hundred dollar bill!"

Let's go back to that same mall for definition #2. When I drive to the mall here in Raleigh, North Carolina, there are many different ways to travel. In fact, here in Raleigh, it seems like any road you take will eventually lead you to the mall. However I travel, I always manage to "find" the mall. It's a known destination and "there are two paths you can go by, but in the long run there's still time to change the road you're on." (Oops, **warning**… heathen rock and roll reference! I'm showing my age.) In other words, because I know where I'm going, I can **find** my way there.

The third definition of the word "find" is a bit more abstract. Imagine you're in college. (For some of you that's a reality!) On the first day of classes, your professor hands out your syllabus and announces that one of your assignments will be to hand in a paper on the last day of class. He tells you how long the paper must be and gives you a suggested topic. You have all you need in order to be successful: a length, a topic, and a deadline. However, without putting the work into creating the paper, you will never be successful. That's what this third definition of "find" is really all about. In our illustration, you will "find" your completed paper as you research, outline, and write the rough and final copies. The paper is **found** as it is created.

So, which do you think it is? Is Lemuel's mother telling him to keep his eyes open to find the wise wife as she passes by in the crowd? Is she telling him that the wise wife is a known destination and Proverbs 31 therefore is the list of things that he will find in that woman? Or, is she saying that definition number three is the way in which Lemuel will find his wife.

Here's the answer for you. In the original Hebrew language, the word "find" is definition #3. Let me explain. Definition #1 is never the way a wise mother would counsel her son to find a wife. Discovering a spouse through happenstance is the same as crossing your fingers and hoping for the best. In the same way, definition #2 doesn't work either. For the excellent wife to be an already developed, already known destination implies one simple but disqualifying truth… She's already married! I don't think any loving mother would counsel her son to pursue someone else's wife!

The choice of the word "find," as defined in definition #3, is no mistake and in fact, it paints a beautiful picture of the marriage relationship. In essence, Lemuel's mother was telling him this: "Son, here are the goals and character qualities that will embody an excellent wife. You, son, must help to develop your wife into this woman!" The goal wasn't for Lemuel to "find" an already developed wife, but to seek a young woman with a teachable heart and a desire to grow and change in order to bring glory to God. Isn't that lovely? God isn't laying out a laundry list of things we must do to be excellent, rather He has compiled qualities that women should grow into as they flourish in the home environment provided by their husbands.

The onus is on our husbands to help us grow. It is they who are tasked with encouraging us, providing the tools we need for growth, and freeing us to use our gifts for the good of our families and our communities. The Proverbs 31 woman is indeed strong, and wise, and a faithful steward, and a compassionate mate, mother, and friend, but she becomes those things as her husband helps her to be "found." Now don't get me wrong here, although Proverbs 31 is written to a man, and although the onus for developing an atmosphere where such a woman thrives is our husband's responsibility, that certainly doesn't give us a free pass to live in any way that we choose. The Proverbs are didactic wisdom

The Proverbs 31 woman is indeed strong, and wise, and a faithful steward, and a compassionate mate, mother, and friend, but she becomes those things as her husband helps her to be "found."

literature, (how's that for a fancy term) or in other words, literature that is meant to impart wisdom. When it comes to Proverbs 31 and the teaching found therein, I think this is the message for women: Wise Up!

No, Proverbs 31 isn't a list of things you must "do," but it is a template for who God would have us "be." The Proverbs 31 woman doesn't gain her praise for specific acts, but for the loving heart behind those acts. A heart that is hardworking, loving, merciful, compassionate, wise, and others-oriented. A heart that prompts practical acts in order to love others well. A heart that ultimately desires to be "found."

May I Meddle For A Moment?

Which leads to an important question, and one that I need to ask. *Ladies, do you want to be found?* Are you willing to allow your husband to encourage you to grow and change to be more like Jesus? Are you an eager participant in your own spiritual growth? Are you prepared to be challenged by your husband? Or, do you respond to his attempts to "find" you with anger, pride, and an unwillingness to change? Have you made it so painful for him to bring challenge and accountability into your life that he truly longs to live on the corner of the roof? (Proverbs 25:24)

This next section is all about respecting our husband's role as the person God has placed in our lives to challenge us to growth, and to hold us accountable to change and transformation. This may be a challenging chapter for some of you. It may make you uncomfortable. In fact, it may be me that you want to run over in the church parking lot by the end of the chapter. May I ask you to simply read with a teachable spirit and moldable heart?

I understand… Honestly I do! I was raised by a mother who proudly proclaimed herself a feminist and who announced to the world that no man, and especially not my father, was going to tell her what to do. I saw the tragedy of her unhappy life and I brought the paradigms and practices that she taught and modeled for me into my own marriage. I promise you… It never brings joy and contentment. God's way is always better! Let me remind you again, this isn't about your husband, his decisions, or his accountability to God. This is simply about you and how you can live in a way that honors and glorifies your Savior and trust me, He's worth it!

Please allow me to share one final thought about Proverbs 31 and Lemuel's mother. Most scholars believe that Lemuel is another name for Solomon. As you'll recall from the Old Testament, Solomon's mother was Bathsheba. Bathsheba became David's wife after her first husband, the valiant warrior Uriah, was placed on the front line of the battlefield. He was placed there because David wanted to ensure that he would be killed in battle. He wanted Uriah dead because Bathsheba was carrying David's child from their adulterous relationship. Now here, in Proverbs 31, Bathsheba is instructing her precious son about the importance of a virtuous wife.

In verse 12 of Proverbs 31, Bathsheba says this about the virtuous woman that Solomon is to "find": *"She does him good and not evil all the days of her life."* If any woman understood the reality of doing her husband evil instead of good, Bathsheba did. Because she didn't refuse the King and stay faithful to her husband, Bathsheba assisted in signing Uriah's death sentence. I'm convinced that Bathsheba spent sleepless nights considering the type of wife she had been to Uriah, and now, here in Proverbs 31, she makes it clear to her son that such actions are not the behavior of an excellent wife.

Bathsheba spoke from painful past experience and what she learned the hard way has been placed in scripture for our good. The wise wife desires to be "found." She's willing to do whatever it takes to be a wife who "does her husband good and not evil." She's willing to say no to life's temptations in order to say yes to her husband and ultimately, her God.

Who's The Boss?

When my daughter, Emma, was just a little girl she was incredibly independent. (Still is… I don't know where she gets it!) Any time I gave her instructions or asked her to complete a task, she would put her chubby little hands on her hips and announce to the world, "You're not the boss of me!" I may not say those words to Steve, but sometimes my attitude is telegraphing that sentiment for the whole world to see. (Except it's not my hands that are chubby…) I never, not even once, asked Emma to do something that she couldn't do or that wasn't the right thing for her at that moment. She just hated the idea of doing something that wasn't her idea and at her initiation, regardless of whether or not it was the right thing for her.

Honest, your husband isn't the enemy! He doesn't ask you to do things just to be bossy. He doesn't suggest changes in your life because he wants to be in control. He doesn't challenge your attitude and hold you accountable to spiritual growth because he has nothing better to do! Remember, part of man's role is to be the initiator and that includes initiating the conversation with you about areas of needed changed. I'm absolutely sure that our husband's would rather eat tree bark than challenge us wives, but if they are to obey God, they need to embrace their role. If we are to obey God, we need to let them embrace that role without making their lives miserable! Want to check it out for yourself? Read Ephesians 5:22-24, Colossians 3:19, and I Peter 3:1-6.

I don't know about you, but I wouldn't want my husband's job. It's hard enough humbling myself and accepting direction and correction, I surely wouldn't want to be the one accountable to God for correcting and directing appropriately! If our husbands are to take their role as our accountability partner seriously, they are choosing to carry a heavy load. In Ephesians 5, verses 25 to 28, husbands are admonished to love their wives in the same way that Christ loves the church. The scripture goes on to say that husbands, just like Christ, must present their wives as holy and blameless. Talk about a serious command!

Steve and I were married in 1984 back in the days when writing your own wedding vows was all the rage and we included this section of scripture in our vows. May I just tell you that the whole idea of Steve presenting me to God as holy and blameless seemed not only improbable, but impossible, as well. Both Steve and I found the concept hilarious and we couldn't get through the vows at our rehearsal without cracking up. In fact, the pictures taken during the ceremony show both of us biting our lips to keep from laughing.

I'm fairly certain that God doesn't think the idea is funny. In fact, His desire is that husbands would love their wives so carefully and considerately that those women would delight to be challenged to live more like Jesus. We can make it a joy for our husbands to encourage our growth or we can make it a painful and distasteful hardship. The choice is ours!

Check Your Attitude At The Door

Since we've started down this road already, let's continue the discussion concerning our attitudes. How do you respond when your husband brings any kind of challenge or even correction into your life? What's your *first* response? Here's why I ask that last question. After 32 years of marriage, generally speaking, eventually I get to the right response. When I have time to slow down, consider what Steve is saying, remember that he's actually not the enemy, and nail my pride back in the coffin… I respond pretty favorably to his loving direction. However, too often, the first words that fly out of my mouth aren't exactly God honoring. In those first few moments, I can turn a simple request from my husband to speak more kindly to the children into a two hour brawl about all the times he's spoken unkindly, and how the children just get me so upset, and the fact that I'm adopted, and my mom didn't understand me, and the humidity has made my hair flat, and yada, yada, yada!

Have you ever been there? Ever found yourself wasting way too much time trying to undo something you said in haste? I think we all have! But where does that attitude come from and is there any way to keep it from invading our homes and ruining our conversations? I think there is.

Quite frankly, what comes out of our mouths is completely indicative of what is going on in our hearts. Therefore, what comes out of our mouths actually shows what we've been feeding on throughout the day. If we're spending time in the Word of God and allowing what we read to change and transform us to be more like Christ, then when our husbands challenge us to make changes, we'll already be in the mindset of change. We'll have softened hearts that are prepared to be transformed in any way that will make us better servants for the Lord. Conversely, if we've filled our hearts and minds with nothing but busyness, inane conversation with the children, time spent gossiping and small talking with our friends, and garbage from afternoon television.... Well, you can guess what's going to come out of our mouths. Time in the Word is the starting point for success.

However even when we've spent adequate time feasting on the Word, it is still in our human nature to be defensive when we're challenged to consider the choices we're making. After all, "I'm 54 years old and I guess I can make up my own mind!" Sound familiar? I can virtually guarantee that if you're saying those words or even thinking those thoughts, you're headed down a bad road. The truth is this: As believers, we have the responsibility to live a holy life; we don't have the right to do whatever we want! Sometimes, that's a tough pill to swallow, but if we can internalize that truth, then we will be well on the road to developing a soft and teachable heart, eager to make changes in order to look and act more like Jesus.

Now, lest you think I write all this from a position of having "arrived"... As I was writing this chapter, literally sitting at my keyboard, Steve FaceTimed me from his hotel in Paris. In the course of our conversation, he asked me to leave my desk in order to go check something on his computer. As you'll recall, I'm an eye-roller.

As believers, we have the responsibility to live a holy life; we don't have the right to do whatever we want.

Now, I didn't intend to roll my eyes. In fact, I didn't even realize I rolled my eyes, but Steve saw the eye roll and pointed it out to me. At that moment, I had the choice to make his role as my challenger an easy one. I could have asked his forgiveness and assured him that I meant no disrespect. Do you think I did that? No! Instead, I dug in and argued with him. I denied rolling my eyes. I accused him of judging me. Pretty soon, you guessed it, we were having "heated fellowship" over Face Time.

Sometimes I think I'm God's slowest learner. Thankfully, He's patient with me and he's given me a husband who is extremely patient as well. Regardless of their patience, it's time for me to nail my self-righteous pride in the coffin and bury it far, far away. Then maybe, just maybe, I'll accept correction for my really lousy attitudes with an attitude of thankfulness for a husband who cares enough to challenge me and push me to grow. How about you?

Let's Get Practical

May I share just a few practical ideas to help you learn to listen first and slow down before responding hastily? First and foremost, if you know that you're spring loaded to respond poorly no matter what your husband says, pray without ceasing. There have been times that I've had to start my day praying for a teachable heart and then repeated that prayer over and over throughout the day. Prayer can change our hearts in ways that, "I've got this under control" just can't.

Secondly, when your husband is speaking to you about some area of challenge or change, look him in the eyes. Again, I'm an eye roller. Trust me, rolling your eyes when your husband is speaking to you is not going to do anything good for your marriage! Make eye contact and hold that eye contact. And oh yeah, don't do it with your "angry eyes!"

Thirdly, fold your hands. I know you're thinking, "What in the world does folding my hands have to do with listening to what my husband is saying?" Actually, it has a lot to do with it. Folding your hands is a great focusing activity. Especially if you tend to interrupt or formulate your rebuttal before he's even done speaking, folding your hands will slow you down and make you think before you speak.

Finally, repeat back a brief summary of what you heard your husband communicate to you. Don't repeat it word for word! I promise, if you try to do that there is just no way you'll be able to do it without adding a sarcastic intonation to the words you don't agree with! When you repeat back the gist of what you heard your husband say, you can be sure that you heard him correctly. There have been many times that after hearing him out in this type of respectful way, I have been able to ask Steve if I could take some time to consider and pray about what he had communicated to me or requested that I do. When my demeanor toward him was respectful, he was always happy to give me that time, and often, when I later came back to him and shared more information, he changed his mind about what he was asking. However, if I rolled my eyes, or interrupted, or responded defensively, invariably we ended up in an argument and the good he was trying to bring about was derailed by miscommunication and hurt feelings.

Don't Shoot The Messenger

When it comes to this area of respecting our husband's role as someone who can hold us accountable, I really believe that too often we think of our husbands as Public Enemy #1. He's really not your nemesis, ladies! Remember, this is the guy who looked so cute when he was a little scruffy and wore that flannel shirt that smelled like "him." This is the same guy that said he liked long haired girls while we were dating and guess what… We grew out our hair. This is the guy that we never wanted to hang up on or say goodnight to at the end of the day. He loves you and wants what is best for you. He's Not The Enemy!

I know it's hard to humble yourself and allow your husband, or anyone else for that matter, to point out your failures. However, we all need that type of tough-love sometimes. The book of James makes it crystal clear that although we can look into the Word of God and see our weaknesses and sin appetites, too often we walk away from the Word and immediately forget what we "look like." (James 1:22-24) Jeremiah 17:9 goes even further when it says this: "The heart is more deceitful than all else and is desperately sick; who can understand it." In other words, when we follow our own hearts, our own inclinations, and our own ways we are setting ourselves up for spiritual failure. What a blessing, then, is a faithful husband who will lovingly challenge us and walk beside us as we seek to pursue Christ-like change in our lives.

Help Me Lord, I'm Married To The Guy Up Front!

For those of you who are pastor's wives… Sisters, I feel your pain! When your husband is your pastor, there's an extra level of pride eradication that has to happen. So many times, "Pastor Steve" would preach a message that affected me deeply. I would sense the conviction of the Holy Spirit and I would know that my heart was being challenged to grow and change. Then came the invitation. My husband always gave two invitations, one for salvation and one for accountability in personal growth. As soon as the piano player began to play the invitation song, my inward battle would begin. I knew that God was prompting me to raise my hand during the invitation, but to do so would mean that the pastor, aka my husband, would know that I was under conviction. That extra layer of accountability just caused me so much inner turmoil. Can you tell how hard God has had to work to help me hate my pride? Steve used to jokingly tell people that God had him marry me because there are just some women who need a pastor 24/7, and I'm one of those women. He was probably right!

Dear pastor's wives please don't let pride or fear of accountability keep you from responding to the prompting of the Holy Spirit. We'll talk about learning to be thankful for our husband's words of conviction in the chapter on gratitude, but for now, may I simply encourage you to embrace God's humility program and accept it as just another way He lovingly calls you to put-off pride and put-on a humble and teachable spirit?

It's Parenting... Not Babysitting

Besides not being your enemy, there's something else your husband isn't and it fits right into this chapter. Your husband is not your children's babysitter! It drives Steve nuts when women say that their husband is home babysitting. No he's not… he's home parenting. Do you know why that bothers my husband so much? It's because "Daddy the babysitter" is a not-so-subtle message that our society has embraced. When that is how you view your husband, you're definitely not going to respectfully receive any challenge or correction from him when it comes to raising the children.

There is a reason that God gave your children two parents. It's because it takes both the male brain and the female brain to parent appropriately! Yes, we spend more time with our children, but that doesn't make us the experts who knows instinctively what is best for those children. When we disrespect our husbands by refusing to allow them to set out the direction of the child training, or by refusing to consider their concerns and ideas as valid, we hurt not only our marriage relationship, but the security of our children, as well.

Sometimes, I think our husbands must think we women are schizophrenic! On one hand, we claim that we want them to be more involved with their children. We maintain that it is their job to lead the family and make sure that we're all headed in a positive spiritual direction. We nag (gently, of course) when we don't think the family and time spent together is the priority it ought to be in their lives. Then, when our husbands do take charge, when they share some changes that they feel ought to happen, when they make plans to do things together… We balk! We disagree with the changes they ask us to implement. We disregard the things they ask us to do. And, unless their new plan fits perfectly into our already-in-place plan, we're unwilling to accommodate them and

Your kids need their dad's input and believe it or not… sometimes you just don't know what is best all of the time!

make it happen. Is it any wonder that our husbands abdicate their roles and just go watch the sports channel?

I'm speaking as a fellow struggler here. As you'll recall, my husband is on the road quite a bit. That means that much of the time, I'm in some sense acting as a single parent. When he was in the Navy, he left on nine-month deployments. For nine months I ruled the roost. I was the Queen of my domain. I called the shots. Then… he came home! I used to tell friends that I was a submissive wife, but only when Steve was deployed. (That's a not so funny joke!) When Steve came home from deployment I really struggled to let him in on the parenting decisions. After all, I knew the children better than he did. I'd put their schedules and routines into place. Who was he to think he could "mess up" my finely tuned and well-established household?

I'll bet you can just feel the overwhelming pride that gripped my heart and directed my attitude. You can probably guess the atmosphere it caused in our home, as well! Our husbands don't have to "earn" the right to parent their own children and they also don't have to "earn" the right to challenge the decisions we're making in the parenting realm. When we send the message that our husband does have to earn that right, whether it is a verbal or non-verbal message, we are treading on thin ice by disrespecting him and setting our entire family up for failure. Your kids need their dad's input and believe it or not… sometimes you just don't know what is best all of the time!

Especially when it comes to parenting our teenaged daughters, Steve's insights and input have been invaluable. It's one thing when our daughters are cute little girls and they think that mommy is just wonderful. However, when those same dear little angels become young women, often we find ourselves in fruitless and circular arguments that are really just female-on-female violence. As much as I don't like it at the time, I'm thankful that Steve steps in and takes me aside to point out the ways that I'm contributing to the issues. Honestly, sometimes I can be so catty with my girls! Definitely not a relationship-builder and not what I want to model for them as a Christian woman.

In His Absence

Perhaps you do a great job following through on what your husband has expressed as his desire for your family when he is present, but how do you do when he is not at home? It can be tempting to live by two different standards, but to do so is a terrible choice. If your children learn that it's important to hold certain standards when dad is home, but permissible to disregard those standards in his absence, you can be certain that they will treat your instructions with the same level of disrespect. We'll be, in effect, training our kids to be hypocrites; children who behave one way in public, and another way when no one is looking.

I was at a conference recently when a mother came to talk to me about this very issue. She was concerned that her daughter didn't have a good relationship with her father. I asked the mother some questions about her husband and she shared with me that he had laid out very clearly the goals he had for their homeschooling days. He had also communicated to both his wife and his daughter that he thought it was very important that the house was locked when he was gone for the day.

After sharing these facts with me, the mom went on to say that she and her daughter thought the father's rules were just silly. She said that although he wanted their homeschooling to follow an orderly progression during the day, she thought it was more important to be spontaneous. She added that both she and her daughter thought the locked door rule was ridiculous and that as soon as he pulled out of the driveway, they made a point to unlock the door and laugh together about their "disobedience to dad." Is it any wonder that the daughter has a poor relationship with her father?

For the good of our families, whether or not our husbands are home to see what we are doing, we need to hold firmly to the standards that he has set in place. Yes, we need to communicate and discuss those standards. We need to give our husbands input about how the day runs most effectively. However, we do not have the freedom to give the appearance that we are following through with what has been decided on when in fact we are disregarding his wishes.

Are You Asking The Hard Questions?

Sometimes, we don't ask our husbands what they desire because quite simply, we don't want to know. If they haven't said it aloud, then we can give ourselves the latitude to do whatever we want without feeling guilty. Ladies, is that really how we want to live our lives? For sure, our children are watching how we live and for most of us there are others watching as well. Do you live such a life in your relationship with the Lord? Although there are plenty of "thus saith the Lord," commands to guide us in the scriptures, there are just as many decisions that we must make based simply on biblical principles. Just because there isn't a specific prohibition doesn't give us the freedom to do whatever we want! I guarantee that if you live your life only following your husband's explicitly stated desires and commands your children will do the same in their obedience to you. Look out!

Breaking Out Of Our Comfort Zones

It's easy to dwell on the part of challenge and accountability that is hard or seems negative to us. But another way that our husband's can fulfill their role in our lives (if we'll let them) is as they encourage us to stretch and grow. Again, our husbands know us better than anyone else. They see our strengths and weaknesses in action. Who better, then, to give us just the push we need to step outside of our comfort zones.

Think about it. If your mom or your best friend told you that they saw a special gift in your life, how would you react? I think most of us would excitedly begin to daydream about how we could put that gift into action. But what if your husband was the one to make the suggestion? Would you react as positively?

For years, I daydreamed about writing books. However, with eight children to feed, clothe, homeschool, and clean up after I just never found the time to write. (Go figure!) I outlined books in my head and thought through progressions and plotlines. But I never, ever wrote any of it down on paper! The only writing I did complete during those years was the funny little stories I wrote for the children and our annual Christmas letter. Five years ago, Steve began to encourage me to write. Every day, (at least it seemed like that to me) he would ask how the writing was going and he'd urge me to just plug away and keep going. Thanks to his encouragement, I completed my first book. That book was entitled, In My Seat, and today's it's sold over 20,000 copies. Unbelievable!

Steve saw my heart's desire and used his role as my closest ally and accountability partner to push, prod, and shove me outside of my comfortable little "mom" life. Today, he's still my biggest cheerleader. Often, he'll read excerpts from my books aloud during conferences and publicly praise me to the audience. Sometimes I just want to sink into a red-faced puddle of embarrassment, but it is his words of encouragement that keep me writing. I'm so thankful that God taught me to trust and act upon Steve's counsel over these many years and that he didn't give up in the beginning when I was a less than eager recipient of what he had to say.

How about you? Is there some area of giftedness that your husband has been encouraging you to develop? Are you willing to trust that God can show *him* ways that *you* could be used to serve the Kingdom of God? Are you willing to trust his assessment of your gifts and talents? What a wonderful gift we have in husbands who push us to be our best and to continually be growing in ways that perhaps we've never even considered. As they carry out their responsibilities as your challenger and accountability partner, you'll grow and God will be glorified. It's truly a win/win situation!

Are You Up For A Challenge?

I want to challenge you to do three things. First, if your husband never engages in a conversation regarding your children or how your children are being trained, ask him for his opinion. It may be that he doesn't have the self-confidence to voice his opinion because he's bought into the world's lie that he is just the "dumb" dad. If that is the case, you can encourage him and let him know that you value his opinion. However, he may be silent because of how you've responded to his input in the past. In that situation, you will need to seek his forgiveness for your previously poor responses and assure him that you truly do want his opinion. Remember, when he shares his opinion it is important to listen and be receptive. It may not be what you want to do, but God gave those children two parents!

Secondly, ask your husband if there is anything he hasn't verbalized about how you're running the home or raising the children that you should know. Make sure he understands that your desire is to honor him even when he's not at home, so you want to be sure that you know not just his spoken wishes, but those things he inwardly longs to see happening at home. Believe me, he'll feel loved, respected, and appreciated by your questions.

While those first two questions might be bit intimidating because the answer might challenge the status quo and point out your own shortcomings, this third question should make your heart excited. Ask your husband what special gifts and talents he sees in your life. Ask him to help you to brainstorm ways that you could develop those talents. Then, tell him that you are eager to be challenged and you really want him to hold you accountable to moving outside of your comfort zone by asking you periodically how it's going.

Once you've asked these three questions, put what you have discovered into practice. As you're making changes in your home or in child training practices, be sure to esteem your husband's desires to your children. Don't behave as though the world is coming to an end because daddy is "so demanding!" Instead, talk to your children

When we are willing to humble ourselves and receive our husband's counsel, correction, challenge, and call to accountability in our lives, we will open the door for God's blessings to flow in.

and help them understand what a blessing it is to have a dad who cares so much about your family. Tell them how it brings you joy to carry out his wishes even when he's not at home. Your positive attitude will reap great fruit in the lives of your children and I think you'll be delighted to see their relationship with their father bloom and grow.

When we are willing to humble ourselves and receive our husband's counsel, correction, challenge, and call to accountability in our lives, we will open the door for God's blessings to flow in. God can use our husbands, the ones who see us and understand us the most, to be instrumental and initiate sweet growth and change in our lives. I have seen over and over again that when I am open to receiving what Steve has to say *to me*, and then willing to act on it in order to grow and change, he is eager to receive counsel *from me* as well. The New Testament speaks of husbands and wives submitting to one another in love. That mutual submission is made easier when we are first willing to humble ourselves, put away our pride, and eagerly seek our husband's loving direction.

WHAT THE HECK? PART 2

MEN AND WOMEN AND THEIR STUFF

Some of the greatest differences I've discovered between men and women come in the form of their "stuff." Whether it's cars, or clothing, or tools, we opposite sexes just aren't on the same page!

What is it about guys and their cars? I don't care how old or young my men are they've just got a "thing" about cars. I remember when my youngest was just two-years old and learning to talk. (He is Guatemalan, so not only did he have to learn to talk after being in foster care, he had to learn to talk in English.) I worked with him every day on the important words like: **Mommy** and **Is** and **Beautiful**. Do you know what that kid's first word was? Muffler! Only he said it like this: Muff-a-ler. Every time a noisy car drove by, from the back seat I heard this angelic little voice whispering Muff-a-ler. Pretty soon, he'd advanced to "This car needs a muff-a-ler." He was just born with car craziness running through his blood!

My conversations with my boys about cars generally sound like this:

Me: I saw a car I really liked today.

Steve: What kind of car was it?

Me: Blue.

As you can probably guess… I drive them nuts! Virtually every day, I find myself in a conversation with one of the boys about which car I'd prefer to have if I could have any car in the world. When I say a blue Jeep they're horrified and have to try to convince me why some uber-fancy, ultra-expensive sports car is just a MUCH better choice. Hey, they asked… I like Jeeps!

Guys have an uncanny ability to notice when something has happened to one of their cars. I never notice little, inconsequential (to me anyway) dings and scratches on the car. Heck, if it still runs we're all good, right? Steve, on the other hand, will be sitting at dinner and I'll watch him get this terrible look on his face. Up he'll rise from the table and the next thing I know he's headed out to the garage. Pretty soon he comes in and says, "How could you not notice that door ding?" (Ummm…I wasn't looking?) I swear the man sees scratches in his sleep!

Once upon a time there was a wife named Megan. She was fairly well known throughout her small Maine town for always having a large iced coffee. (Heavy cream and 2 sweet 'n low, please) One day while backing out of the local coffee shop in her "Big Blue Van-thing" she was distracted by her eight precious children and barely, just barely banged into a handicapped parking sign. She checked the van and hey… it was still running so life was good. She arrived at church where her distracted pastor-husband greeted her without even noticing the minimal, teeny-tiny, barely there; hey it wasn't really her fault damage. Sadly, she attended church with some of those car-loving alien species men. Those Ratfinks took bright silver duck tape and put a big X right over the dent. Guess what her precious pastor-husband noticed as soon as he exited the church? Ugh… men are such tattle tales!

Have you ever noticed how much guys "baby" their cars? Steve cleans, and shines, and polishes his beloved sports car. He never leaves trash in the car pockets or empty cups in the cup holders. The same cannot be said about how he maintains his office. For him, a clean car is a happy car and he wants my car to be "happy" too. Not me! I keep a very clean house, but the car… Not so much! With eight kids in our big 15 passenger van most of the time my vehicle looked very much like a pre-school Sunday School class had vomited all over the floor; gluey cotton balls, sticky finger paints, and glitter (that gift from Satan) included. I've finally achieved clean car status, but I'm afraid it's only because all I have left is teenaged boys. (Clean, but stinky!)

Speaking of noticing little things about their cars… How is it that Steve can "miss" that he's left the dirty ice cream scooper on the kitchen counter overnight, but if I drop one little, itty-bitty cough drop wrapper on the floor it's like he's developed laser vision.

Have you ever noticed that they're just as uptight about their tools? I'm a minimalist when it comes to kitchen tools. I'd rather chop my own foods than use a food processor. I use basically the same knife for 99% of the cooking I do and that works fine for me. However, occasionally I have a kitchen job that just needs a tool I don't own. Lids that need to be pried off, meat that needs to be pounded, or some other little job that just calls for something different to accomplish the task.

I've never been able to understand why my husband gets so upset about me "borrowing" something from his tool bag if it will help me get the job done. I mean really… What's the big deal? I'd let him borrow anything he wants from me, although of course he never wants anything of mine... He wasn't happy about me pounding the steaks with his hammer. He grumbled about me using his screwdriver to pry open the pickle jar. But things really came to a head over his silly chisel.

We were young marrieds living in our first house. Finally, no more apartments; we were the owners of our first castle! (Figuratively speaking) I noticed one of the drawer pulls in my new kitchen was just spinning loosely. I tried to use a butter knife to fix it, but the knife was just too thick. That's when I remembered the really skinny screwdriver looking thingy in Steve's tool bag. I found the chisel, rammed it in place, and fixed that drawer in no time! I was actually pretty pleased with myself. That is... until Steve came home and that uncanny "man sense" drove him to look in his tool bag. How was I to know that chisels are honed to a delicate edge? Gosh! Men are just so picky about their tools...

Speaking of men and kitchens... What is it that makes men find their wives so irresistible when they're cooking? Regardless of the meal I'm preparing, Steve just can't resist canoodling in the kitchen. I originally thought that was just a "Steve quirk," but I've noticed my son-in-laws are infected with that same cuddle-bug!

It's funny, but for knowing so much about their own stuff, men can be just clueless when it comes to female possessions. For years, Steve called everything that I wore that wasn't pants or shorts, a dress. I'd patiently explain the difference to him between a dress, a jumper, and a skirt, but still every time I came out in a cute skirt or motherly jumper, he'd say, "What a nice dress!" Just today, he told me that he remembers skirts as half-dresses, but he always has to remind himself which half they're supposed to cover-Wow!

Come to think of it, some of these differences really work out well for me. I love having a man who knows his cars. If it weren't for him I'd probably be miserably driving around town with the top down in my blue Jeep. That would be terrible, right? If he knew too much about women's clothing, I might be suspicious. Yeah, I'll take him just the way he is although sometimes I catch myself thinking:

WHAT THE HECK?

CHAPTER 7

GIVE THANKS WITH A GRATEFUL HEART

"Gratitude is the memory of the heart."
Jean Baptiste

"Silent gratitude isn't much use to anyone."
G.B. Stern

Just for the record, I love Thanksgiving. Like I *seriously* love it! All those other holidays are nice, but Thanksgiving is the one that fills my heart with joy, my tummy with yummies, and our dining room with everyone I can possibly manage to invite over and squeeze around the table. For whatever reason, Thanksgiving is the only holiday that we can generally count on Steve being home to enjoy it with us. I'm guessing that most pilots prefer Christmas off and for us that works out perfectly. All of my kids feel the same about Thanksgiving. For the married kids, they know I'll never pester them to choose us for the holidays, but they all always manage to get home for Thanksgiving. Actually, the year we moved to North Carolina, we arrived at our new home two days before Thanksgiving.

As always, all the big kids and their spouses converged the next day eager to celebrate and absolutely convinced we needed to eat all of our regular, and honestly quite time consuming, favorites. I struck a bargain and those kids unpacked my whole house while I made pumpkin pies, from-scratch cranberry sauce, and their "must have" Mom's homemade stuffing!

I don't just love Thanksgiving for the food, fellowship, and atmosphere though. I really love stopping in the middle of our busy year to just push pause and spend a little time focusing on what it is that makes us thankful; what people or things are filling our hearts with joy. I try to mix it up from year to year, but our Thanksgiving meal always ends with a time of each person around our table sharing grateful thoughts.

This past year, we had a completely full table. Our guests included my daughter's college roommate, Anne, who is a beautiful single girl, and five single young men ranging in age from 15 to 26. I gave each person a blank card and they listed three things for which they were thankful and then signed their name at the bottom. We collected the cards and Steve read them aloud. Every single one of those boys had listed Anne being at Thanksgiving as #1 thing they were most thankful for that day! Needless to say, Anne had a great time and I'll have to contact all those boys because she's already arranged to come back again this year.

Planting Seeds Of Thankfulness

Thankfulness breeds more thankfulness and I'm always encouraged to hear the things for which my loved ones are grateful. When they share thankful thoughts about each other, I watch their relationships flourish and our family bonds grow even stronger.

That beautiful relational strengthening is the exact reason we should be overwhelmingly generous in expressing thankfulness toward our husband for the things he provides, the way he leads, and most importantly, who he is.

Are you characterized by having a heart of contentment? The dictionary definition is so simple, it says this: a state of happiness and satisfaction. Our level of contentment sends a strong message to our husbands regarding how well we think they are providing for us. A man who cannot seem to make his wife content will never be a man who feels respected and affirmed. Conversely, when our men are confident that we are content in our homes and circumstances, they will be able to work without the stress of always feeling as though they just can't do enough to please us.

I feel sorry for our husbands sometimes. We can be awfully hard to please. On one hand, we communicate that we just don't have enough stuff. We need more clothes, or books, or food, or whatever we seem to be lacking, and therefore our husbands must work harder and longer to provide those things for us. Then, when they are gone from home working harder and longer to provide what's lacking, we change course midstream and communicate our displeasure in their continual absence from the home. "How," we ask, "will the children ever survive without

A man who cannot seem to make his wife content will never be a man who feels respected and affirmed.

a father who is more involved?" Poor guys! They can't ever seem to get it right.

Now I know that scenario isn't true for all of you, but as I've sat across the counseling table from many women, that's exactly the complaints I've heard them utter. We need to understand that when we learn to live lives of contentment, we will build up and encourage our husbands. If we choose to live lives of "never enough" we will only succeed in tearing our husband's down and bringing discouragement into their lives. The wise wife is a builder, as you'll remember from chapter two.

Contentment and thankfulness really go hand in hand. When we learn to be content with all that our husbands and the Lord have provided for us, we will soon be filled with thankfulness for those very things. When we learn to express thankfulness verbally and through our actions, we will become even more content with all that we have been provided.

The apostle Paul, in the book of Philippians, stated boldly that he had learned to live with much and with little, in abundance and in poverty. How did he learn to live in such a way? I believe it was because he recognized everything he had as a gift from God. With that recognition came thankfulness and thankfulness bred contentment in his heart.

Thankfulness and contentment don't come from having "enough" or being comfortable in our present circumstances. Instead, thankfulness and contentment come from a heart that has found its peace in Jesus Christ. Thankfulness and contentment are directly related to the depth of our personal relationship with the Lord. When we are walking in intimacy with Him, we will be able to recognize the blessings and gifts He provides and we will be able to echo the sentiments of the Apostle Paul.

Content or Coveting?

How would your husband answer this question: "Is your wife content?" Would he be confident that you are thankful and content for the life that you are living? Or, because of your words or actions would he lack that confidence? If a husband is unsure of his wife's contentment, he will lack security and self-confidence regarding his ability to provide. If you haven't verbalized that you are thankful for what you have and how you are living you can't be sure that your husband knows deep in his heart that you are content.

If you're not sure how your husband would answer the question above, may I encourage you to spend time expressing your thankfulness to him? Look around your home and ask God to give you eyes to see all of your blessings and a heart that is filled with gratitude. Discontent can be eradicated as we replace coveting with contentment and grumbling with gratitude. One of the best ways to express your thankfulness for what your husband has provided for you is by being a good steward of those things. Taking good care of what you already have will affirm to your husband that you don't take his work on your behalf for granted.

It took me a long time to realize that when I didn't treat our possessions with carefulness, Steve felt disrespected and dishonored. He finally spoke up and told me that when I treated items as though they were disposable by not taking good care of them, he felt as though I didn't appreciate all of his hard work. For him, the amount of time he had to spend away from home to provide for his large family felt worthless when we weren't good stewards of what that work provided for us. Quite frankly, some of our possessions weren't the nicest, but they were all we could afford at the time and Steve had worked hard to procure them for us. Treating them poorly was more an indication of my heart problem than the actual worth of the items.

Consider your stewardship. Are there areas of your home or items in your home that you do not treat with the care that is necessary to keep them working or in good condition? Are you discontent and wanting more but unwilling to care for what you already have? If so, I promise that your husband isn't missing the message that you are sending him. Whether you ever utter the words aloud or not, he'll know you're not thankful, grateful, or content with what you have.

Contentment never comes from having everything that we think we want; rather contentment comes from a recognition that God has provided all that we need. Simply getting more stuff won't make you thankful and content. Some of the unhappiest and most discontented people I know have more "things" than they can even manage. Contentment has little to do with what we have and everything to do with our inward attitude. Contentment and thankfulness will make your marriage strong! Remember I told you that Steve was excited about how capable I was? Part of being capable has always meant living contentedly with what he has provided for our family.

Contentment never comes from having everything that we think we want; rather contentment comes from a recognition that God has provided all that we need.

What Do You Say, Dear?

I've always made it a point to thank Steve for everything he provides. I never want him to think I take his hard work for granted. How about you? Do you thank your husband for all that he provides for you and your family? When we don't take the time to express our thankfulness, we run the risk of seeming entitled or ungrateful.

Honestly, I'm not sure what makes saying, "Thank you," so difficult for some of us. I think of "thank you" as a carefully wrapped package with a beautiful bow on the top. (Something I can't do in real life, but at least I can imagine what it looks like!) When our husbands unwrap that package the gift inside says, "I noticed! You show me love so well!" Such a gift would make anyone feel appreciated, noticed, and loved in return. Why wouldn't we want our husbands to feel that type of gratitude?

One of the things I've found as I've spoken to ladies about this topic is concerning to me. Many women seem to feel that their husbands owe them everything they're given. I don't know if it's because they just feel entitled or if it's that they think their husbands are so lucky to have them, but for whatever reason, they balk at giving thanks because they feel as though what they've received is an obligation and as such, not worthy of their gratitude. What a horrible attitude that is! As believers, we should be known for our overflowing and gracious words of thankfulness. Our doctors "owe" us their service, yet we say thank you to them. Our waiters and waitresses "owe" us their service and we thank them anyway. (At least I sure hope you do!)

There are so many verses that speak of thankfulness and giving thanks. However, when it comes to this area of withholding thanks when thanks is due, the passage that always comes to my mind is Luke 6:38.

"Give, and it will be given to you. Good measure, pressed down, shaken together, running over, will be put into your lap. For with the measure you use it will be measured back to you."

In other words, when it comes to thankfulness and the expressions of a grateful heart, we will receive back exactly in the way that we have given out. I don't know about you, but when my husband expresses gratitude for the things I have done for him, I feel appreciated. When he is thankful for his relationship with me, I feel loved. When he notices the ways that I serve him and acknowledges those things with a glad heart, I am encouraged to do even more for him in the future.

Thankfulness begets thankfulness and gratitude will produce a crop of joy in your marriage. Don't be stingy! Take every opportunity to show your thankful heart. Say it loudly, say it often, and say it with your words, your actions, and your whole heart… Thank you!

It's The Little Things That Count

The wise wife isn't just thankful for the things that her husband provides, she is also thankful for the ways that he serves the family. How does your husband serve you? Just like each of us will serve our husband's differently because of their different needs and personalities, the way our husbands serve us will be different as well. I have some friends whose husbands serve them by cleaning or cooking and they're very thankful for those services. I know other husbands that send their wives away once a week to just get some alone time. Again, what a wonderful gift those husbands are providing for their spouses.

For me, it's the little things that Steve does for which I'm so very thankful. For instance, he has always made sure that my car had gas in the tank. That may not seem like a big deal, but when I had eight children thirteen and under still living at home the thought of running out of gas and having to walk down the highway with all of the children in tow was frightening to me. Especially since we lived on an island in Maine and there were no gas stations on the island! You'd better believe I was quick to express my gratitude every time I saw the full sign on my gas gauge.

When I was expecting our fifth child, Steve took over the grocery shopping for me. Of all of my responsibilities, grocery shopping is the only one that I truly hate! I don't know what it is about going grocery shopping, but I always end up tired, cranky, and freezing cold. (Don't they have heat in grocery stores?) I couldn't thank Steve enough for freeing me from that job while I was waddling around carrying Nate.

While expressing thankfulness and gratitude will do great things for our husbands' hearts, it also has some added bonuses. The more thankful we are for the things our husbands do for us, the more they will want to lovingly serve us. Now obviously, we don't express gratitude just so that we'll get more, but that is a sweet side effect of showing thankfulness. As well, for those of us who have children, showing our husbands honor and respect through thankfulness will model that same attitude for our children to emulate.

It is so easy for children to develop an attitude of entitlement. Recognizing that what their father provides and the things that he does for them are expressions of his love for them, not something that is owed to them, will help suppress those attitudes of entitlement. I'll be honest with you, when it comes to my children I truly believe that when we had less, they were far more content. When all eight kids were living at home, and especially for the years that we opened our home to another family, we lived basically paycheck-to-paycheck. We never lacked food or clothing, but there just wasn't a whole lot of extra money that we could afford to spend on non-necessities. My kids knew that if we needed clothes, we would be shopping at the Thrift Store on half price day. They didn't mind at all that I baked most of our bread and that there were weeks we ate a LOT of egg dishes because I could get fresh eggs so cheaply.

Today, with just two kids at home, we just have more money at our disposal. It's easier to say yes to the extras that my boys say they want. Now, more than ever, it's important for me to model thankfulness for those boys. It would be so easy to take all that we have for granted, but the truth is that their father still works just as hard as ever. He hasn't slowed down just because there are less of us living at home. He still works hard to provide things for us, and he works just as hard to serve us in the ways that we find most meaningful. We have a lot to be thankful for and it's my job to lead the way in expressing that thankfulness.

Someone To Watch Over Me

Thankfulness doesn't end with what our husbands provide for us or how they serve us though. How about how they protect us? One of the biblical roles our husbands are called to fill is that of the protector. There are many different ways that our husbands provide protection for our families. The most obvious way would of course be how they protect us physically. I'm thankful that my husband makes sure that our home is a safe place. He has always chosen where we would live so carefully. He knew that he would be away often and he never wanted me to feel nervous or afraid in our home. When I remember to thank him for his physical protection it affirms that I notice the watchful way he cares for me.

Steve has also been a great protector when it comes to my time and my relationships. I'm a bit of an over-achiever when it comes to filling needs for other people. In fact, around our house the kids and Steve sometimes call me "helium arms." You know, when a request for help is made it's like I just can't help myself; my arm automatically goes up in the air. Without Steve's reminders to keep my priorities in order, I would run the risk of over-committing to things that steal time from my primary priorities; my husband, my family, and the ministry opportunities that God has laid out before me. Sometimes I chafe at Steve's insistence that I slow down and think before committing to one more thing, but I'm thankful that he still works hard to keep me on course in spite of my impatience with the process. Keeping me in check could be a thankless job if I didn't remember to show gratitude for how he cares for me… even when I don't like having to say No to an opportunity that looks inviting to me.

When it comes to friendships, Steve's protection has kept me from some very bad decisions. More than once, God has given him the discernment to see that a friendship in which I was involved was not heading in a godly direction. To be honest, this area of his watchful care in my life has been the hardest to accept. I am extremely trusting and I don't ever want to think that someone I care about could be leading me down a bad path or using me without really caring about me. The times that I have refused to allow Steve to protect me by counseling me about my friendship choices have been some of the most hurtful times of my life. It's hard to admit when he is recognizing something that I, quite frankly, don't want to see, but protecting my heart is just as much a part of his role as protecting me physically.

Does your husband know that you're thankful for his protection? We should never take such tender care for granted, but instead we should express verbally our gratitude for his watchful and loving care over us. In our culture, being a husband who protects his wife isn't necessarily applauded or seen as a positive thing. We are told that women are to be independent and being cared for by a man is stifling and controlling. In God's eyes, nothing could be further from the truth. Just as Christ lovingly protects His church, the husband is to emulate His Savior and lovingly protect his wife. Our words of thankfulness will make his job sweet and fulfilling, regardless of what the rest of the world has to say about him.

Just The Way You Are

The wise wife is a wife who makes sure that her husband knows she is thankful for him just the way he is and just for whom he is. True thankfulness is never tinged by the word, "but." You know what I mean… "I love you, but I just wish you'd________." It's so important that our husbands know we are thankful for them even if they stay exactly the way they are with no changes.

Which characterizes you, praising your husband's strengths or pointing out your husband's weaknesses? It's so easy to get into the habit of always pointing out the weak areas of our husband's lives.

We are squeezed by a culture that is trying to feminize men and make them more like women.

When this is the pattern of our communication, we can be sure that our husbands will feel like defeated failures. However, if we are quick to point out their strengths, they will have the encouragement they need to be successful.

Sometimes, we aren't thankful for those things that make our husbands different than us. We are squeezed by a culture that is trying to feminize men and make them more like women. If we begin to buy into those cultural lies, the very things that make our husbands manly will become repugnant to us. When that happens, it won't matter what they do, they will appear as failures in our eyes.

Think about those things that make your husband uniquely himself. Have you thanked him for those things? My husband is an over the top idea guy. From the moment he wakes up in the morning until he falls asleep at night, (instantly... like the second his head hits the pillow) he is popping with new ideas. I, on the other hand, am a methodical and organized thinker. I love plans, and lists, and structure, and routine.

In the first years of our marriage, if you had asked me whether or not I was thankful for Steve just exactly the way he was, I'm not sure what my answer would have been. To be perfectly honest, for years his "idea guy" personality drove me absolutely nuts! No, I didn't want to sell everything and go live on a houseboat! (Just one of his many "we could save so much money" ideas) I balked at his ideas and often just pretended that I couldn't hear what he was saying! I wasn't exactly the poster girl for the wise and respectful wife.

God has really changed my heart over these 32 years and now I'm so thankful for the man He gave me. Without Steve's big idea to plant a church, Cornerstone Baptist Church wouldn't exist. Without Steve's big idea to minister to families, Characterhealth wouldn't have changed so many parent's and children's relationships. Without Steve's big idea (and some strategic pushing and prodding) I certainly wouldn't be a conference speaker and writer. Without Steve's big ideas, so many of the areas of ministry that God has opened to our family wouldn't exist and so many people would not have been touched by the gospel.

Today, I can truthfully thank Steve with all my heart just for being exactly who he is and I don't even want him to change! Even during those times that our family has faced trials because Steve was battling with God, I've learned to be thankful. I'm thankful because as God was dealing with Steve, He was also dealing with me and teaching me to be thankful for a man who wrestles with God. Sometimes, as wise wives, we have to be willing to put up with hard times and struggles so that our husbands can have the freedom and space they need to grow and change to be more like Christ. Even in those trials, we can be thankful. I know many women who wish for husbands who had any desire to grow as Christians. When our husbands are growing, even if it shakes up our comfortable status quo, we should be thankful and express that thanks to them. Hearing that we are thankful for their growth, rather than annoyed by the uncomfortable circumstances caused by their growth, will encourage them to produce even greater spiritual fruit.

I'd say "Yes" all over again!

Finally, we are living wisely when we make it a point to express to our husbands how thankful we are to be married to them. We've all heard the joke about the old farmer who when asked how often he told his wife he loved her said, "I told her when we got married and nothing's changed. Why would I tell her again?" That joke may get a laugh, but if that's what is happening in your marriage relationship it surely isn't very funny.

Steve tells me frequently how thankful he is that we are married. Actually, he tells me that he's thankful that I haven't run away because of all his big ideas! He thanks me for going on this adventure called life with him. I am acutely aware that sometimes I can be a real handful to deal with. I know for a fact that sometimes… I'm just a pill. But… and this is a big but… I also know, without any doubt, that Steve Scheibner is thankful to call me his wife! I know it because he tells me! Have you told your husband that you're thankful that **he** is your husband lately?

Don't be satisfied to simply be thankful and content on the inside. Don't assume that your husband knows you're thankful for what he provides. Don't just hope that he knows you're grateful for how he serves you. Don't forget that his protection over you is a sweet gift of love. Don't get so caught up in wanting him to change that you neglect to be thankful for who he is right now, today. Don't keep any of those thoughts to yourself… verbalize them to your husband. Tell him often how thankful you are for him. Keep a running list of all that you have to be grateful for and communicate those things to your husband. A marriage, built on a foundation of contentment and thankfulness will be able to withstand the storms of life. Now that's something to be thankful for!

I never want to point out a problem area without giving some sort of practical solution. A "to-do," if you will. Several years ago on Father's Day, I came up with an idea of how we could honor Steve and show him just how much we love and respect him. (Now, before you give me too much credit here, I must tell you that I thought of this on Father's Day morning and when I had no money to help the kids get him a gift. At first it was just a cheap alternative...) I asked the kids to join me and we made an extensive list of all the things about Steve for which we were thankful. The list truly ran the gamut from funny to very serious. One child was thankful that his dad let him win at Go Fish. (Sometimes) A daughter was thankful for the way he had helped her step out of a not-so-healthy relationship. My son was thankful that his dad was always forgiving, regardless of what blunder that son had just committed. Yes, just like yours, my kids blow it sometimes!

I thought the list would be a sweet way to end our dessert after the fancy Father's Day dinner I had prepared for Steve. I had no idea just how meaningful it would actually be to him. I was stunned to see my husband sitting wiping tears from his eyes. After the list was read, he said this: "Guys, that makes it all worthwhile. All the work and all the striving to make our family special; it's all worth it when I know you're grateful for it."

May I encourage, no...urge and exhort you, to make just such a list for your husband? Perhaps you may want to include the children in the list making, but maybe not. Maybe your husband needs to hear it just from you. Your words of thankfulness and gratitude may be all he needs to know and to understand that yes... It's worth it!

CHAPTER 8

HONORING YOUR HUSBAND THROUGH PRAYER

"Prayer does not change God, but it changes him who prays."
Soren Kierkegaard

"Beware in your prayers, above everything else, of limiting God, not only by unbelief, but by fancying that you know what He can do. Expect unexpected things 'above all that we ask or think.'"
Andrew Murray

Far beyond the words that we say, the services that we provide, the thankfulness we show, and the respect we offer to our husbands is the power of the prayers we utter on their behalf. In fact, I'm convinced that if we could simply nail down our prayer lives, all of those other areas would merely fall into place.

Oh how I wish that I could tell you that I am a prayer warrior who intercedes effectively on behalf of my husband. The truth is that prayer has always been a struggle for me. It isn't that I don't want to pray; it is simply that I find myself distracted or shallow in my prayer life. It is only as I'm maturing (and I have the grey hair to show for it) that I'm finally beginning to understand what the Apostle Paul meant when he enjoined us to "Pray without Ceasing." (I Thessalonians 5:17) More and more, I find myself just talking with God throughout the day. He's become my "go-to" Person for all of my fears, joys, concerns, and busy thoughts. My heart's desire is to make intercession on Steve's behalf an integral part of those daily conversations with God.

Keeping It Real

It's been said, "Prayer changes things." I absolutely agree with that statement, but I would submit that the first thing that prayer changes is my own heart. So often, I've come to God in prayer expecting him to change my husband and make him fit into the mold I've prepared for him, and instead God has changed my understanding of what the mold should look like in reality. True prayer takes the focus off of my desires and me and aligns my heart with God and His desires. True prayer goes so far beyond the shallow "be blessed" and "be with" prayers that I run to with little thought or consideration.

You know what I mean by "be blessed" and "be with" prayers, right? "God, be with Steve while he travels." "God, be with Steve as he works." "God, let his decisions be blessed." "God, let his work for this family be blessed." The list of shallow prayers could go on and on. If we want to truly pray for our husbands, we're going to have to put some thought into the process and get our own agendas out of the way.

I have found it helpful to begin my prayers for Steve with prayers for myself. Does that seem strange to you? The prayers for myself go something like this: "God could you keep me out of this? I'm not sure that what I want for Steve is what you want for him, so if I'm out of line would you deal with me first?" One thing I've learned for sure after years of trying to pray effectively for my husband is that what I envision as best for Steve and the ways I'm sure he needs to grow and change are miniscule compared to what God has in store for him. God's plans are always bigger and better than mine! God's call to change in Steve's life is always God-centered, while too often my prayers for change are Megan-centered. I don't really want Steve to change to fit into my plans or dreams for our family; I want him to change in the ways that God knows are best.

So if it's okay with you, let's travel this chapter together and join forces as we learn to pray as wise wives. Just think of what our men could accomplish with the consistent and persistent prayers of their wives to undergird them and go before them to the God of the Universe! Let's get started.

Thy Will Be Done

Obviously, first and foremost, a wise wife should pray that her husband lives a life that is according to God's plan and timing. When Steve and I were first married, I was convinced that he should be a pastor. After all, weren't all spiritual men called to the pastorate? My prayers on his behalf were very much, "God, would you hurry up and convince him!" prayers. I coupled those prayers with some insistent nagging and well-timed disapproval. (Sigh, eye-roll, and huff) Imagine my surprise when Steve just didn't get the word from God and get on board with my plan for his life! Many times of "heated fellowship" later, I finally realized that God wanted me to get out of the way.

Steve was only accountable to walk faithfully according to God's plan, not mine. Your husband is only accountable to walk according to God's plan, not yours! It takes us removing our hands from the driver's wheel of our husband's lives for them to be able to hear God's voice clearly. Our prayers for them regarding the way they live should simply be prayers that they would hear God clearly and obey Him completely. If they can do that, they will be well pleasing to God and then it's our job to get rid of our expectations and be thankful for our husband's commitment to obedience. Ephesians 4:1 urges all believers to live a life worthy of their calling. That calling comes from God, not us His little helpers!

Sometimes, God's sense of humor is painfully obvious in my life. And I do mean painfully! Fifteen years after I tried to convince Steve that I knew exactly what God wanted him to do and that was to get out of the Navy and go be a pastor, God called Steve to the pastorate. Ladies, I may just possibly be the most fickle woman alive because when Steve told me what he felt God was calling him to I responded so poorly! Fifteen years previously, I'd been raring to go and I just wanted us to get on with ministering together in a church setting. When it finally came about in 2000, I was scared to death. I knew Steve would be a great pastor, but by then I had developed a much more accurate understanding of myself. Me, a pastor's wife... No way! I didn't even play the piano. Fifteen years later and God still had to get me out of the way so that Steve could walk faithfully with Him.

It's You And Me, Buddy

If our marriages are our most important relationship on earth and since they are to be an accurate representation of our relationship with Christ, a wise wife will pray for the health of her marriage. I always pray that God would be glorified in our marriage. Can I just tell you that often that glorification comes through iron sharpening iron? Or, in our case, sandpaper rubbing against a stubborn knot in the wood. (Yep, you guessed it the knot's name is Megan!) Every wife should pray that her husband would be equipped by God to lead effectively in the marriage. That's a great prayer. The problem comes when we begin in our prayers by instructing God about exactly how we think that "leading" should go. Trust me, how God would have your husband lead, and how you desire to be led, are often two very different courses of action!

Ephesians 5:25-29 gives a clear pattern for how husbands should lead their wives. If we pray that scripture over the life of our husband, without interjecting our own interpretation of the scriptures (around here we call it the RMV or the Revised Megan Version) we can be confident of praying God's will for our husband. A husband who lovingly leads his wife by following the scriptural model will truly bring glory to God.

Wisdom In The Trenches

Every day our husbands face trials and temptations. Even if they're involved in full-time ministry their days may be filled with discouragement and disagreement. Actually, after having seen both sides of the coin, secular employment and full-time ministry, I would say that a Christian environment might at times be even more hurtful for our husbands. Especially if they are involved in any type of counseling, the probability of ending their workday with one or more people upset with them is extremely high!

Remind your husband as he heads out the door for work that you are praying for him. Let him know that while he is at work, you are praying at home that he would lean on Christ throughout the day. Then do it! To tell our husbands that we are praying when in actuality we are just thinking about their circumstances or even just going about our day without talking to the Lord is dishonest. If you say you're going to pray… Do it! Psalm 46:1 is a great scripture to pray for your husband. Pray that he would know, without a doubt, that God is a refuge and strength for him just at the moment that he needs Him.

All believers need God's discernment, but our husbands especially need to have an extra measure of biblical discernment. As the leaders in our homes, they are responsible before God for so many areas. They need discernment in the decisions they make regarding our finances. They need discernment as they determine how to practice generosity as a family. They need discernment as they lie out goals for the family and develop a plan to reach those goals.

I know we want to help our husbands with all of those decisions and we can and should help him. However, before we ever offer our discernment, we must pray that he would have God's discernment. This is one area in which Steve confidently knows I pray faithfully for him. I so desperately want him to make good decisions for our family so that we are walking in God's perfect will. Because he knows that I pray so diligently in this area, when I do have an opinion concerning a decision he is making he trusts what I have to say to him. That doesn't mean that he always takes my counsel, but he is always willing to listen. He trusts that just as I am praying for discernment for him, I am also praying that God would give me His discernment as well.

Discernment and wisdom go hand in hand, so as we are praying for our husband's discernment we should also pray that they would be seeking wisdom. As they spend time in the Word of God, He can open their eyes to receive His guidance. Just a thought here, ladies… I've said before that it's much easier for us to find time to spend searching the scriptures. It is imperative that your husband has time to immerse himself in God's Word if he is to have the wisdom and discernment that he needs to make God-honoring decisions. Do you allow him that time? Do you make it easy for him to slip away to meet with God? Or, do you preoccupy his time and make him feel guilty for spending any of his home time away from you? If you want him to practice God-honoring decision making, you will have to give him the time and space he needs to do so.

James 1:5 tells us that God gives His wisdom generously to anyone who asks for it. You can be certain that God longs to generously supply your husband with all of the wisdom and discernment he needs for every circumstance in which you find yourselves. If your husband is facing a particularly hard decision, persistently and consistently petition God on his behalf concerning that decision. Be like the persistent widow and don't hesitate to run to God over and over as a faithful advocate for your husband.

You can be certain that God longs to generously supply your husband with all of the wisdom and discernment he needs for every circumstance in which you find yourselves.

All You Have To Do Is Ask

At one point in our marriage, I made the decision to fast once a week. I'll let you do your own research on fasting, but I can tell you that I chose to fast because I was seeking to learn how to pray more effectively. During my times of fasting, I kept a three-ringed binder on my kitchen counter with notebook paper and dividers in it. Each family member had their own section of the notebook, as well as a section for our friends. I encouraged everyone to write down their prayer requests with the promise that each Monday, the day I fasted, I would pray for those requests. I kept track of the results of those prayers, and sometimes, even when the folks who had requested prayer had long forgotten about the need they'd written down, I had the blessing of sharing how God had answered that prayer.

Steve consistently wrote prayer requests in that notebook. Often, his requests were things that we hadn't even discussed, but they laid heavy on his heart. Sometimes, because of his role as Pastor, he couldn't write specifics, but he could communicate to me that he needed extra wisdom for a difficult situation. What an incredible joy it was for me to be able to pray for him so specifically. I'm afraid that before the notebook existed there were probably times he needed that extra prayer support, but he was afraid that if he shared the need with me I'd try to jump in and fix the issue. I quickly learned how much better it was to let God be the "fixer" of his problems and the "filler" of his needs.

I promise you, ladies, I can talk a problem to death! However, I can never pray too much about a need in my husband's life. God is delighted when His women care enough about His men to bring them before His throne. Prayer is one of those areas that your husband may never know for sure whether or not you're praying for him. Tell him that you are and share your prayers and the answers to those prayers with him.

In Sickness And In Health

It almost goes without saying that we should pray for our husband's health, job situations, safety, etc. With a husband who is an airline pilot, you'd think I'm right on top of that whole praying for safety thing. Truthfully, it's easy to take our husband's life, health, and safety for granted sometimes. When everyday just flows into the next with no troublesome illnesses or accidents, it's easy to just assume God's hand of protection.

Just a couple months ago, I was reminded once again to pray for my husband's safety. Since 9/11, he hasn't really had any frightening airplane incidents, however that changed in the month of February. One Sunday night, Steve left from New York for a flight to Paris around 6:00 pm. Before he left, as always he gave me a final phone call and then we signed off until the next day when he would Face Time me from his final destination. About three hours after his departure my phone rang. When I answered the phone, Steve was on the line. He'd actually been trying to call for several minutes, but because all of the kids were over and we were playing a very loud game of Pie Face, no one heard the phone. (I love that game!) During a momentary lull in the action, I realized my phone was ringing. When I saw it was Steve, my heart sank! There was no way he should have been calling me at the three-hour point of a nine-hour flight.

Sure enough, there had been an airplane incident. In fact, some of you may have seen it on the news. Steve's plane, with him seated at the controls, had hit something called a wall cloud that hadn't shown up on anyone's radar. Although he managed to turn and divert the plane from flying straight into the wall cloud, the plane took quite a hit and seven passengers ended up in the hospital. I could tell Steve was very shaken up which is almost unheard of for him. We talked and prayed over the phone, but when we hung up God continued to speak to my heart. He reminded me of how lackadaisical I had become in the area of praying for Steve's safety. Just because he hadn't ever had a bad accident, I just assumed he never would. Praying for him was my privilege as his wife and I had been squandering that privilege.

Please don't think any part of your husband's life is too small or inconsequential to take to the Lord in prayer. Your prayers will undergird your husband and they will help you to hand your concerns for him over to God. My shoulders aren't big enough to carry the responsibility for everything that could happen to Steve on any given day, but God's sure are!

What's In It For Me?

Regardless of whether or not your husband knows about your praying life… God knows! God will use those prayers to bless your marriage and bring about godly growth and maturity in your own life. Have you ever noticed how hard it is to stay angry with someone while you're praying for them? Prayer softens our hearts and helps us to develop compassion. As well, when we're worried or fretting over a decision that our husband must make, prayer can calm us down and help us to entrust both the decision and our husband to God.

Sometimes, there is just turmoil in our marital relationships. God can use our prayers to help us think clearly and make an effective plan of action to deal with the turmoil. There were times early in our marriage that Steve would leave for a flight with unresolved conflict still hanging between us. Once he left, I would begin to walk around the house planning in my mind how we would now be nothing more than roommates. I would think through just how we could cohabitate without ever really having to speak to one another again. (Pretty mature of me, eh?) Invariably, the Holy Spirit would begin to draw my heart to prayer. Annoyingly, the Spirit would begin to remind me of all the good qualities that Steve possessed, which in that moment I was just choosing to ignore. The more I prayed in obedience, the more my heart was drawn to my husband. Every single time by the time he arrived home, I was soft as putty and ready to restore. God's good that way even when I want to hold on to my stubborn stiff-necked pride.

It Never Hurts To Ask

The wise wife is quick to seek her husband's help through prayer also. All the women I know are such deep wells of thoughts and concerns. This means that it's just so easy for us to overflow with worry and fear. God has given our husbands the privilege and responsibility to help us carry those burdens. He can use our spouses to point us back to Christ and to "real life" thinking.

Once upon a time there was a very naughty Scheibner child. That child cheated on his spelling test and shocked his teacher. (Me!) Two hours later, his teacher discovered that while that child was sorting socks (Home-Ec class) he'd stolen all of the change from the "you left it in your pockets and it now becomes mine" jar on the dryer. Oh the horror! Besides being shocked at his behavior I had to deal with my thoughts, which quite frankly were running amuck. By the time Steve got home from work I had convinced myself that the unnamed child would soon flunk out of school, steal more money off of the dryer to buy drugs, (because OBVIOUSLY if he flunked out he'd have to do drugs) and end up in prison. I was tearful just imagining all of us going to visit on Sunday afternoons; me dressed from head to toe in black and all of his sisters in their matching black jumpers.

Scenarios like that are exactly why we need to run to our husbands and seek their redirecting prayers at the first sign of thoughts run amuck. Don't pass Go… Don't collect 200 dollars… Just go ask for prayer! When it comes to prayer, don't try to be the Lone Ranger! Allow your husband to minister to you through prayer. Just as your prayers for him will availeth much, (James 5:16) his prayers for you will be a balm for your soul.

This next suggestion is just that… a suggestion. A wise wife will pray with her husband. Praying together as a couple is one of the most profitable things you can do for your marriage. There's just one problem, your husband has to want to pray together as well. Obviously, we can't justify nagging our husbands about the need to pray together. Besides, that wouldn't work anyway. We'd end up in an argument, (heated fellowship again) and wouldn't want to pray with each other when it was all said and done.

What can you do if your husband isn't interested in praying with you? Wait for it… Pray About It! Prayer is a gift divinely presented to us by God, Himself. It is His desire that as we pray together our hearts would be joined together with His. With that in mind, a prayer that seeks God's help in building a husband and wife prayer life is a prayer that is certainly within His will. I can't promise that the answer will be immediate, but you can trust the Holy Spirit to intercede on your behalf. In the meantime, just keep on praying!

Although I've shared a few scriptures in this chapter that we can use in our prayer times for our husbands, I'd like to close out the chapter with two particular passages that really summarize those things we know are God's will for us to pray about. When you are unsure what to pray or when you've begun to slip into the "be blessed" or "be with" syndrome of praying, here's a great place to land in order to pray effectively.

The first passage is found in Ephesians 1:16-19 and the Apostle Paul says this:

> *(Paul) Do not cease giving thanks for you, while making mention of you in my prayers: that the God of our Lord Jesus Christ, the Father of glory, may give you a spirit of wisdom and of revelation in the knowledge of Him. I pray that the eyes of your heart may be enlightened, so that you may know what is the hope of His calling, what are the riches of the glory of His inheritance in the saints, and what is the surpassing greatness of His power toward us who believe. These are in accordance with the working of the strength of His might.*

What a precious section of scripture and what a precious way to pray for our husbands. These verses really cover all of the things we should pray for them! It reminds us to pray with thanksgiving. Then it goes on to offer prayers for wisdom, knowledge, and an enlightened heart. The verses end in encouragement as we pray for our husbands to truly understand the power that is theirs because of their relationship with Christ.

The second passage is much like the first, but it adds even more depth to our understanding of what God desires for our husbands. (And honestly, all of our friends and loved ones) This passage is found in Colossians 1:9-12 and again it is the Apostle Paul speaking.

For this reason also, since the day we heard of it, we have not ceased to pray for you and to ask that you may be filled with the knowledge of His will in all spiritual wisdom and understanding, so that you may walk in a manner worthy of the Lord, to please Him in all respects, bearing fruit in every good work and increasing in the knowledge of God; strengthened with all power, according to His glorious might, for the attaining of all steadfastness and patience; joyously giving thanks to the Father, who has qualified us to share in the inheritance of the saints in light.

As in the Ephesians passage, these verses remind us to pray for our husbands to be filled with wisdom and discernment and also to realize what God has provided for them. However, this section of scripture goes on to lead us as we pray for the daily fruit that God desires to see evidenced in our husbands' lives and the fruit that they will display to others; fruit like steadfastness, patience, and thankfulness.

Only God knows the exact growth that needs to happen in our husband's lives in order for them to live more faithfully for Him. As we pray the scriptures over their lives, we can be confident that we are stepping out of the way personally and simply coming before the throne of God as ambassadors beseeching Him on behalf of our husbands. It is God then who sees the needs and brings about Spirit-led change in our husbands' lives. Even when

Praying together as a couple is one of the most profitable things you can do for your marriage.

the change isn't what we think should happen, we can trust that God's change is the perfect change; not just for our husbands but for us as well.

I can think of no better way to honor our husbands than through praying for them. Ask the Lord to show you how to pray effective prayers for your husband. Allow prayer to soften your heart and give you great compassion for the man you married. Take his concerns to the only One who can truly bring about the answers and solutions he needs. Allow your husband to minister to you in your vulnerability as you transparently share your joys, concerns, and fears with him. Build unity and oneness as you walk together toward God through prayer.

Prayer… What a precious gift from our Father who sees our needs and loves us so very much!

CHAPTER NINE

WHEN LIFE ISN'T SUNSHINE AND ROSES

It's always helpful to have somebody to help buoy in difficult times and problem-solve with and to share the marvelous moments with as well.

-Jane Poynter

This chapter is going to be a little different from everything we've discussed so far. Up until now, the emphasis has been on us; how we think, how we react, how we serve, pray, honor. We've looked at the importance of a great attitude and how that affects every area of our marriage. We've talked about sinful habits that can trip us up and positive actions that will bring us blessing. Purposefully, the focus has been us, us, and us! Now, however, it's time to turn the corner and focus on our husbands.

Some of you may be thinking to yourselves, "What the heck took you so long! It's about time we talk about his issues in this marriage!" There's a reason we aren't getting to this topic until chapter eight and the reason is all about… You guessed it… Us! If we started talking about our husbands and all of the ways that they fail us back in Chapter one, it would have been so easy to miss the primary message of this book. Let me remind you of that message just one more time:

You cannot change your husband and he is not your responsibility! You can only, through the help of the Holy Spirit, change yourself, in order to bring glory to God and blessing to your marriage!

All of the chapters leading up to this one were chapters intended to help you build the spiritual strength you will need each day as you strive to live as a wise wife. Every time you choose to bless your husband rather than retaliate with verbal missiles, you will need strength. Every time you choose to think of his needs rather than look out only for yourself, you will need strength. Every time you pray for your husband rather than grumble under your breath about "that man," you will need strength.

Every time you choose to bless you husband rather than retaliate with verbal missiles, you will need strength.

Think of the previous eight chapters as your workout routine! Just as the Proverbs 31 woman girded herself and strengthened her arms for her physical labor, we are girding ourselves and strengthening our hearts for the daily work involved in choosing to honor God and bless our husbands.

As I mentioned back in chapter 4, this book is intended for "normal" wives in "normal" marriages. (Honestly, I'm not even

Every time you choose to bless you husband rather than retaliate with verbal missiles, you will need strength.

sure what normal looks like anymore, but we'll use that term for lack of a better word.) In the same manner, chapters 1-7 dealt with our attitudes and thought lives during "normal" times. You know what I mean… When life is just going along in it's regular routine. When our days, although never stress-free, are kind of same-old/same-old. Sometimes, those days may seem boring or uninteresting, but truly, those are the days that give us the greatest opportunity to build that spiritual and emotional muscle we're going need in order to make the difficult choices to continue living wisely when we're facing hard days.

I think of it this way… We're much like athletes when it comes to training our hearts for wise living. (Athletes without the cute uniforms, six-pack abs, and golden tans, but athletes nonetheless!) If you've ever been around an athlete in training, they're a whole different breed of human. My oldest five children were not athletic. They loved to sing, and act, and read, and create. In other words, they were like their dad! My youngest three, on the other hand, have lived and breathed athletics since they could walk. All three of them thrive on competition and they are willing to put up with hours of boring, mundane, repetitious practice in order to be the best they can be in their chosen sports. And yes, they got it from their mother!

I've spent more hours than I care to remember sitting by the side of soccer fields, timing on pool decks, and cheering by the baseball diamond. Now, my youngest is a record holding long jumper and I've added track meets to my resume. Ever been to a track meet? Or, worse yet, a cross-country meet? Mind-numbing… But even the most boring meet, even the most mundane soccer game is more exciting than watching a team practicing their sport. Whether it's lap after lap in the pool or swing after swing of the bat, there's just nothing very exciting about watching my kids when there's no competition involved.

Regardless, it is as they faithfully put in those mundane, repetitious hours that my kids build the strength and muscle memory they need to compete and excel. You see, all that repetition isn't just about getting stronger; they are actually training their muscles to do exactly what they need them to do… Even When They're Not Thinking About It! Whether there are distractingly cute girls in the bleachers or not, when my son hears the crack of the bat and sees a ball headed to the outfield, his muscles instinctively take over and help him make the play. When my youngest is obsessing because his track cleats are too tight and his track shorts are too short and the gun goes off… his muscles instinctively send him flying down the track.

Think about it… Tiger Woods trained every single day to have the perfect golf stroke. Day after day, week after week, year after year he practiced the same stroke over and over again. Because of his constant training on those boring days with no competition involved, he developed an unbelievably perfect stroke. He almost couldn't swing the club wrong if he tried. His repetitive practice made him a model golfer. Sadly, Tiger Woods didn't apply the same daily training to his moral character and now he finds himself a shamed and unhappy man.

Although most of us have no need to perfect a flawless golf swing, all of those normal, mundane days we face are the perfect training ground for us to develop strong and well-defined spiritual and emotional muscles. As we make biblical choices for our marriage, day after day and hour after hour, we will be training ourselves how to react in any and every situation. We compete how we train, and in the marriage realm we react and act the way we have practiced each day. The goal is to be so practiced in our biblical choices that our first response is a Christ-honoring response. That doesn't happen without consistent and daily repetition of good choices! If we allow ourselves the freedom to "take the day off" from honoring God in our marriages, we will never build the spiritual muscles we need to respond appropriately, and in fact, almost instinctively.

Boring, mundane days are the practice fields for those times when trials rear their ugly heads. And that, my dear sisters, is why Chapters 1-7 focused on us. We alone are responsible for building that spiritual muscle. I don't know about you, but I'd love to have a spiritual six-pack! Just as physical exercise provides us with "happy" endorphins, working out spiritually through time in the Word, prayer, and application of God's truths will build spiritual endorphins. Spiritual endorphins make all of that boring practice worthwhile.

When my kids are getting themselves psyched up for a competition, I'll often overhear them declaring, "I'm going to Beast this one!" They're prepared to succeed in the event because they've built confidence as they trained in their practice times. I want to be more like my kids when it comes to facing hard times; don't you? Ladies, let's do this thing! It's time to Beast those unavoidable trials of life!

Trials will come; they're simply inevitable. James 1:2-3 says:

"Consider it all joy, my brethren, when you encounter various trials, knowing that the testing of your faith produces endurance."

Interestingly, those verses don't say "if you encounter trials," they say, "when you encounter trials." Trials are a normal part of the Christian life and God's intention for those trials is that they would build endurance. That's what spiritual muscle really is... Carefully and prayerfully built endurance. In studying this passage of scripture, I discovered that our English word "various," when used to describe our trials, should actually be translated as the word, "multi-colored." In other words, no two trials will look exactly the same. The trials that God allows into our lives will look different for each of us. Sometimes, trials will come that simply involve us. Sometimes, trials will be a family matter. And, sometimes, trials will come because of our husbands. It is how we train in those boring "trial-free" times that will determine how we persevere through the difficulty of trials.

So now, this chapter is about dealing with "husband-induced" trials. We're primarily going to look at five different areas of trial that we may encounter in our marriages. Notice, I didn't say "husband-sin-induced" trials. Although one area will deal with husbands who are making sinful choices, often the trials our husbands, and therefore, we face are not self-induced, but rather the inevitable trials that are simply part of existing in a fallen world.

The five areas we will be examining are: dealing with the in-laws, dealing with unemployment, dealing with physical illness, dealing with depression, and finally, dealing with a husband who is living sinfully. Thankfully, most of us won't deal with all five of those areas and hopefully none of us will deal with all five areas at once!

As we prayerfully and consistently practice wisdom in our daily decisions as a wife, we will be preparing our hearts for whatever trial comes our way.

I've spent time discussing marriage and marriage related issues with hundreds of women and these five areas have consistently shown up as predictable areas of strife in so many women's marriages. Obviously there are many other areas of strife that we can face, but in my mind, these are the "Big Five."

We don't need to fear the "Big Five" and anxiously hold our breath waiting for the trial to begin! Instead, as we prayerfully and consistently practice wisdom in our daily decisions as a wife, we will be preparing our hearts for whatever trial comes our way. God, in His infinite wisdom, knows exactly which trials will perfect us and make us more conformed to the image of Christ, so you can trust that when the trial comes, it is ultimately for your spiritual growth!

Before we dive into the first specific trial, I want to share just a couple truths about trials in general. First, our trials are not a surprise to God. Our loving Father has allowed each and every trial that comes into our lives, whether large or small. That doesn't mean that He caused the trial, and it certainly doesn't mean that He takes any measure of joy in our trials, it simply means that He has foreseen the trial and recognizes that it can be used to draw us closer to Christ. Romans 8:28 says:

"And we know that God causes all things to work together for good to those who love God, to those who are called according to His purpose."

I believe that all trials are meant to accomplish two things:

My Good/God's Glory

In other words, it's two sides of a balanced equation. The problem comes when we try to take control of the wrong side of that equation. It is God's responsibility to bring about the good from each trial that comes into our lives. Humanly speaking, sometimes it is virtually impossible to see how anything good can come from hard or hurtful times. However, in God's economy, He sees the end of the chapter. In fact, He wrote the book! He sees the good that will come, perhaps not today, or even tomorrow, but a good outcome nonetheless. We waste far too much time trying to discern, discover, and just plain dig out what "good" is going to look like. When we do so, we too often become discouraged and disappointed. Let God take care of His side of the equation! Watch with great expectation for the good He will bring about! Keep your eyes open to see Him work, and marvel at the wonderful ways He protects, provides, and acts on your behalf.

If God is responsible for bringing about good in our lives as a result of the trials we face, it is then our responsibility to carry out the other side of the equation. Regardless of the trial and regardless of the circumstances in which we find ourselves, we are always, always, always to bring glory to God! In chapter 2, we looked at I Corinthians 10:31 and it bears repeating here:

"Whether, then, you eat or drink or whatever you do, do all to the glory of God."

The trials we face land smack dab in the middle of "whatever you do." In normal times, we are to bring glory to God. In times of great blessing, we are to bring glory to God. And finally, in trials, we are to bring glory to God. When we are so focused on bringing Him glory that nothing else matters, we won't waste our time trying to determine how anything "good" can come from our trial. As we focus on Him and His glory, we'll effectively take the focus off of us, and therefore be a transparent witness for Christ. We'll become a signpost for others, pointing directly to Jesus, as we glorify Him during trials that those who don't know Him would often find unbearable.

Indeed trials will come and yes, sometimes they'll come because of our husbands, but as we trust God to bring about good in those trials, we'll experience growth in our relationship with Christ. And, as we seek to glorify God by our Christlike and biblical choices throughout the trial, God will be honored and our husbands will be blessed. This is exactly what we've been training for ladies! Now, it's time to pull on those spiritual yoga pants and put all that training into action.

When the In-Laws Seem More Like Out-Laws

In my own marriage, and after hours of counseling with couples in all stages of life, it seems as though in-law issues are one of the first major trials that couples face together. If they aren't dealt with biblically, and if a wife doesn't learn how to support her husband while still honoring both his parents and hers, the initial trial can become a life-long issue causing hurt and distance for everyone involved. Some of our saddest times of counseling involved in-laws who were so upset with their adult children that they couldn't speak civilly, thus causing the young adults to cut off the relationship and prevent their own parents from building loving relationships with the grandchildren. Oh my! That should never be the testimony of Christian families!

Regardless of whether the trial comes from your parents or his, a wise wife never allows in-law issues to cause her to dishonor her husband and create a wedge in the marriage. Part of the leaving and cleaving process is learning how to communicate and respond as a team when it comes to each other's parents. Some parents make that leave and cleave process an easy transition as they respectfully observe their adult children's decisions. Those are the in-laws who wait to be asked for advice, instead of simply offering their opinion. Other parents, though, make that process painful and stress producing.

For us, the in-law problems really began the night before the wedding. My mom, who was not okay in many ways, (how's that for nebulous) announced the night before the wedding that if I used the word "submit" in my wedding vows, she would get up and leave. As I said before, Steve and I wrote our own vows and part of the scripture we chose to include was Ephesians 5:22. Guess what word is included in that verse… Yep, submit!

I'm a peacemaker at heart and the last thing I wanted was conflict with my mom the night before my wedding. My husband, however, is not a peacemaker in the same way that I am. He flatly told my mom that the word, submit, would be in the vows and if she wanted to leave, she could. Before I'd even said, "I do," I found myself caught between my soon-to-be-husband and my mom. That was one of those trials that I didn't see coming! I think God knew what a people-pleaser I was and He wanted me to start from Day One with an understanding of the need to respect my husband's decisions and back him up in times of disagreement with my parents. Just more wedding angst… In retrospect, maybe we should have eloped!

Do whatever it takes to turn disagreement into peaceful co-existence and trial into blessing.

Not surprisingly, the pre-wedding conflict was only the first of many conflicts with my mom. Sometimes I wished that Steve would simply give in and do whatever she wanted just to keep the peace! However, despite my qualms, he continued to firmly demand that she respect our relationship and stop manipulating me. Because of the whole "submit" issue, my mom refused to speak to me for the entire first year of our marriage. I would call and speak to my dad, but he always said that talking to me would just cause too much "stress" for my mom. What a painful and heartbreaking year! Can I be honest? In the beginning, I blamed Steve for the trial in which I found myself. I thought if he'd just be more agreeable we could sweep all the conflict under the carpet and everything would be just fine.

After several years of my mom pushing, pushing, pushing and Steve standing firm in his conviction that she needed to respect and recognize our primary relationship, I began to see my mom change. Suddenly, she was speaking words of praise about my husband. She was telling my brothers what a good man he was and how well he cared for me. She was showing him respect, and in return, she was gaining another son. Steve hadn't changed, but my mom had learned to respect his position as my husband.

I'm convinced that if Steve had surrendered to my repeated pleas to just give in and capitulate to her demands, we would have never found ourselves in the peaceful and loving relationship we developed with my mom. Interestingly, when my mom was in hospice care, it was Steve she interacted with the most. She would light up and become much more communicative and less lost in her world of dementia whenever he entered the room. What a blessing to watch!

That lesson of watching my husband respond to my mother has carried over into my parenting. I'm much softer on my boys than Steve. In fact, I'm pretty much a pushover when it comes to my guys. Steve, on the other hand, holds his ground and provides the security they need by not caving in to their demands. I've learned not to intervene with my ooshy-gooshy mom nonsense when he's teaching them lessons of respect and honor.

One of my favorite women ever, Margaret Thatcher, said this about dealing with those who push the walls of respect and authority: "Never appease an aggressor." Sometimes, our parents unfortunately begin to fill the role of aggressors as they try to take on an authority position in our marriages that just doesn't belong to them. Don't try to soften the issue if your husband is setting biblical boundaries intended to protect your marriage!

If there is strife between your husband and your parents, pray about the situation. Ask for God's wisdom in order to discern your role in the situation. Sometimes, we blame our husbands for strife that has really come about because we have refused to abandon our role of obedient daughter, in order to take on the mantle of loving wife. If the issue is you, do whatever is necessary to end the strife and clearly establish marital boundaries.

It could be, however, that your husband and parents just don't get along. What a difficult trial, indeed. Again, pray and ask God to build bridges of communication and trust between both sides. Look for ways to encourage relationship and be especially careful not to stir up the embers of strife by complaining to your husband about your parents or gossiping to your parents about your husband!

But what if the trial you are facing comes about because of one of his parents? We tell our young adults all of the time, "You marry the family, and so choose wisely!" If you've been married any length of time, you know that is absolutely true. Perhaps your father-in-law interferes in your family's decisions. Or, maybe your mother-in-law constantly corrects your parenting style. How are we to deal in a biblical way with the trial of meddlesome or just plain old annoying in-laws?

Romans 12:18 tells us exactly how we are to bear up under this trial. Consider how we are instructed to live:

> ***If possible, so far as it depends on you, be at peace with all men.***

Like it or not, our in-laws definitely fall into the "all men" category, and since that's true, it is our responsibility to find a way to be at peace with them. This isn't a "If they're nice to me, I'll be nice to them," situation, but rather we are to take the responsibility for finding ways to build relationship and peacefully co-exist with them. It's not our husband's responsibility to be the go-between and if we put him in that position the strife will only get worse! The exception would be when his parents are refusing to communicate with you or if they are abusive in their communication. At those times, it's perfectly acceptable for our husbands to step in and protect us and they absolutely should.

Steve had already left for the Navy the first time I spent any significant amount of time alone with his mom. The most memorable part of our first evening together was overhearing her say on the phone, "Oh Stephen's fiancé is here. I think her name is Megan, but it's so hard to remember with all of the girls he likes." Grrr! Needless to say, it was a rough start to our relationship.

You'll remember, when Steve and I got engaged I was a jeans and sweatshirt, no make-up kind of girl. Steve's mom, on the other hand, paid for plastic surgery to upgrade her nose and chin. She wore every kind of make-up you can imagine and she had a rat's tail dyed blonde in the back of her hair. To top things off, she had a tattoo. Now, I'm not anti-tattoo, but she had one back in the days when only sailors got inked! Honestly, on the surface, we had nothing in common!

Beyond the surface we didn't click much better. I was a tomboy athlete; she had been a girly ballerina. I loved sitting by the ocean and staring at the waves; she loved going to the shore to hit up the casinos. I was a new believer trying to figure out this whole "Christian" thing; she was a new believer also, but she still filled her home with dream catchers and read her horoscope every day… Just in case!

From the earliest days of our marriage, she would say to my husband, "It doesn't matter what Megan thinks, she's just your wife. I'm your mother!" The topper came after the birth of our first child. While I was upstairs napping, I heard a tap, tap, tapping sound. Getting up to inspect, I found my mother-in-law carefully lowering all of the pictures in our home. She was about 4'9" and just thought everything was a bit too high on our walls.

Can you understand why I considered her to be one of my biggest trials? Everything about her just bugged me and I didn't hesitate to let Steve, her son, know that I thought she was his problem to deal with. It wasn't that things weren't peaceful between us; they just weren't anything. The relationship was void. Hardly a relationship that brought glory to God and definitely a relationship that caused strife in my marriage.

My relationship with Steve's mom didn't change for many, many years. Oh sure, at times I half-heartedly prayed about my connection with my mother-in-law, but honestly, most of the prayers were some variation of, "Why me Lord? Could you just make her a bit more lovable?" On one of her visits to see the grandchildren while we were in Texas, however, God finally got my attention.

My mother-in-law truly was a believer in the Lord Jesus Christ. Of course, in my estimation she didn't live a life worthy of Him, but nonetheless, she was a Christian. (Wow! Judgmental much?) One of her practices was to raise her hands in worship. We were attending a fairly conservative Baptist church at the time of her visit and I inwardly fretted about her hand raising. I considered asking her not to raise her hands, but that somehow didn't seem right. Instead, I just kept up my ongoing "she's so awkward and annoying" conversation in my head.

We arrived at church on Sunday morning and as the service began, sure enough, up went her hands. You can just imagine me cringing in my seat. But then, I noticed something. On the other side of my mother-in-law sat one of the sweetest and most mature Christian women that I knew. She was a mentor and someone I truly looked up to for advice and guidance. She loved everyone and was always the first to welcome new visitors. And… she had her hands in the air just like my mother-in-law.

I knew it wasn't the normal practice for this dear sister to raise her hands, but she did it to make my mother-in-law feel loved and welcomed. She wasn't seeing the hair, or the make-up, or the tattoo. She just saw a sister-in-Christ who needed to feel a part of the worship that morning. Ugh… Conviction! I don't remember anything else from that service, but I do remember talking to God and making a commitment to love Steve's mom the same way He loved her.

That commitment wasn't easy to keep and it had to begin with seeking forgiveness from Steve for putting him in the middle of a tense relationship between his two women. Then, I asked my mother-in-law to forgive me for not being a better daughter-in-law. (Honestly, I inwardly hoped she'd ask my forgiveness too, but she didn't. For me, it was just another reminder that God takes care of the other person's heart; He wants me to focus on my heart and my responsibility in each relationship.)

** A quick disclaimer here: Just like tattoos, I don't have any issue with raising our hands in worship. The problem was the culture of our church at the time and what I saw as an outward action that didn't match my mother-in-law's daily lifestyle.

How do your change a "trial" relationship into a "blessing" relationship? For my relationship with my mother-in-law to change it meant that I had to learn to love her Just The Way She Was! I began by praying for a heart that was attuned to see the positive fruit in her life. When I stopped complaining about her and began to truly develop a friendship with her, I realized just how hard-working, faithful, and transparent she truly was as a woman. When I began to ask her questions about herself, (there's a novel idea, Megan) I began to see the strong woman who had withstood the pressure of two alcoholic husbands. I started to appreciate the years of labor she put in to raise her son as a single mom. I learned to love her for the sacrifices she made by leaving her family and friends in Detroit, in order to save Steve from becoming involved in the gang culture that surrounded him. Yes, we were still totally different women, but God began to slowly, but surely, build a loving relationship between us.

In the last few years before her death, my mother-in-law and I spoke every morning after breakfast. If for some reason, she didn't call, I missed our conversation! She became my go-to person to share the children's accomplishments and a trusted friend who always encouraged me that my life as a stay-at-home mom was worthwhile. We learned to laugh at our differences and I even let her buy me clothes that as she said, "Weren't old lady frumpy clothes!" At her funeral, I was touched as her friends all shared that when she spoke to them, she referred to me as her "best friend." She's been gone for 10 years now and I miss her terribly!

It makes me sad to think of the years of friendship we missed. On the other hand, I'm so thankful that God opened my eyes to see Marion as something more than a "trial" sent to cause me frustration. Like so many of the trials I've faced, once the focus was finally off of me and my expectations, the trial became a blessing and my heart was changed for the better.

Yes, sometimes the in-laws cause trial and heartache. We can just muddle along in that mess or we can purpose to glorify Christ through a renewed relationship with them. Always, in-law strife causes unhappiness in our marriages. Whether it's our parents or his, discord related to our extended families causes discord in our homes. Don't wait for them to go first! Do whatever it takes to turn disagreement into peaceful co-existence and trial into blessing.

Facing the Unemployment "Time-Out" Chair

Another area of trial that is becoming all too commonplace in our current economic environment is dealing with a husband's unemployment or loss of job. While some husbands may bring about these trials because of laziness or a poor work ethic, more often, our husbands find themselves on the sideline of the job market simply because of company cuts and unexpected business mergers. How do we live wisely during these times of family stress? How do we manage our own fears without heaping a burden of guilt on our husbands?

The trials brought on by unemployment or the loss of a job goes far beyond just dealing with a husband who is home all day. With the loss of income comes a myriad of other problems. We may lose our health insurance. We may not be able to pay our bills and mortgage. We may have to make radical changes in our lifestyle and way of living.

All of these harsh realities are absolutely true, however in the midst of the practical problems is a man who has been wounded in one of his greatest areas of insecurity. For our husbands, providing for us, and ensuring that we feel safe and secure is one of their primary roles. When that role is stripped from them, they are left hurting and carrying a burden of failure. It is at this moment, that we either show our wisdom through proving ourselves to be their greatest ally in the struggle, or we become part of the issue, reminding them of their greatest failure.

Some women have shared with me that part of the trial associated with a husband's job loss is the reality of having their husband home all day and every day. May I encourage you to view that new paradigm as a blessing, rather than as a trial? Don't doubt for a moment that your husband realizes you're frustrated by his continual presence! How lousy it must feel to consider yourself a burden that your family is saddled with all day. Having our husbands home all day is easily changed from a trial into an opportunity just by a simple realignment of our attitude. Instead of begrudging the need to rearrange your plans in order to include your husband, express your happiness that a bad situation (the job loss) has provided a unique opportunity for more time together. Instead of trying to make him fit into the already established family schedule, find ways to enjoy outings or activities that he wouldn't normally be able to take part in because of his work schedule. Make him feel included, rather than communicating the message that you can't wait until he's back to work and out of your hair! Your husband already feels unwanted in the working world; don't make him feel the same way at home!

When I was just a little girl, my dad's roofing company closed due to bankruptcy. I didn't really understand all that meant at the time, but I did know that my happy-go-lucky father was suddenly silent and distracted. For two years, he spent hours outside of our home each day handing out resumes and meeting with executives. Two years is a long time to go without a paycheck! When the holidays came around food baskets were delivered to our door. Again, I didn't realize what those food baskets meant; I just loved the extravagant treats that we found inside them. But for my dad, those baskets meant failure and an inability to provide for his family.

During those two years, I watched my mother belittle my father's inability to get a job. She boasted of how easily she could find a job, yet she never volunteered to go to work. She pointed out how my father's lack of a college education was handicapping our entire family. She complained about what we didn't have and pointed out what our neighbors possessed. She took a hard situation for my dad, and basically made it unbearable. She chose a road of foolishness!

I learned some really good lessons from my mom, but that was a bad lesson I learned from her. I decided, even as an elementary aged little girl, that if my husband ever lost his job, I would be his biggest cheerleader. Watching my father wilt under my mother's condemnation taught me a lifelong lesson.

In 1989, Steve made the decision to end his time with the Navy and pursue a job with the airlines. In those days, every airline was hiring and every pilot we knew was immediately picked up for employment. Not Steve though. Our time with the Navy came to an end and he still didn't have an airline job. For the first time in our marriage, we didn't have a steady paycheck and we didn't really know when we'd have one in the future.

When Steve was pursing an airline job, the hiring process at American Airlines was interesting to say the least. After Steve's initial interview, he was told to call the airline each day at 8:00 am and 4:00 pm to see if he had been hired. Every day we prayed before making the phone calls and every day we waited to hear the news… Yes or no. That went on for weeks with no relief! In the meantime, every day Steve wheeled his woodworking equipment out onto the driveway and he worked on furniture projects in order to make us a little bit of money. He used to joke that those were the days when his best friends were the neighborhood retirees and dogs.

In the midst of waiting to hear from American Airlines, we found out that we were expecting our fourth child. Of course we were thrilled, however I wouldn't be honest if I didn't say the stress level in our home rose considerably. But may I remind you, we fight the way we train and from the time I was a little girl, I had trained my heart for just such a situation. Yes, I was absolutely scared to death. What if he couldn't find a job? What if we couldn't pay for medical care for the pregnancy? What if we couldn't pay the rent

He dwells in the reality of our daily circumstances and in His faithful promises to us.

and had to move out? What if we had to move in with my parents!? So many, "what if" questions, and no immediate answers.

May I share something I learned during that time, and hopefully it will be an encouragement to you if and when you find yourself in a similar situation? My thoughts were consumed with the "what if's" of life and those thoughts were the very means Satan was using to fill my heart with fear and insecurity. God DOES NOT live in the "what if's" of life. He dwells in the reality of our daily circumstances and in His faithful promises to us. His promise for each day is a promise that He will not give us more than we can bear. (I Corinthians 10:13)

In addition, God's grace is sufficient for the exact trial we are facing. It is not, however, intended for trials that "might" happen. That's exactly what the "what if's" of life actually are… Imagined trials that might never come to pass. To give us grace for imagined trials would be to waste grace! Instead we are instructed to take those "what if" thoughts captive and make them obedient to Christ. 2 Corinthians 10:5 says this:

We are destroying speculations and every lofty thing raised up against the knowledge of God, and we are taking every thought captive to the obedience of Christ.

We must learn to harness those unruly "what if" thoughts if we are to be able to minister grace to our husbands in their time of need.

I'm convinced that the only way I kept from burdening Steve with those fearful thoughts I was battling was because for years beforehand I had prepared my heart to deal with job loss. That early lesson I incorporated from watching my mom's bad attitude produced good fruit 20 years later. And that is why it's so vitally important to train ourselves to live wisely during those boring, mundane times of life. When hard times come, and trust me, they will… We'll be ready to face them with courage and faith!

Do you remember when I said that every husband needs a capable wife? In a time of unemployment or job loss, that capability is even more necessary than usual. As we cheerfully show our husbands that we are able to live on a reduced budget, we will reassure their hearts. As we join them in prayer rather than bombard them with our fears and doubts, we will bless them immeasurably. And, as we purposefully remind them of their gifts, capabilities, and strengths, we will embolden them to face their circumstance with courage and hope. What an incredibly important role we fill in the lives of our husbands!

The loss of a steady income is definitely a stressful trial and I'm not trying to minimize the difficulties it can cause in our homes. However, as Elizabeth Elliott so often wrote, we must simply "Do the next thing." Whether that next thing is to tighten our budget, sell unnecessary possessions, or search the Want Ads, the next thing is never, ever, ever to worry about tomorrow! Worry will only make the trial more burdensome and it won't change your circumstances.

God is big enough to bear you through the waters of unemployment. Don't allow the trial to pull you under and swallow you up, but instead, prepare your heart to come alongside your husband and together paddle safely to the shore of God's will for your life. Trials equal growth in our lives and often, the trial of unemployment or losing a job helps us to realign our focus onto those things that really matter in our lives and for the Kingdom of God.

* In looking back over the past few paragraphs, I realized how simple it would be to read about the trials I faced and think I just

knocked them out of the park. (I really love a good baseball reference) Nothing could be further from the truth! It's easy to look back and write about the positive outcome of a trial, but in reality, getting to that outcome had more than its fair share of hiccups along the way. When it came to Steve's unemployment, I really was prepared to respond in a biblical manner. However, as a newlywed with a troublesome mother-in-law, I was probably the biggest whiner baby around. It took time, a little maturity, and a solid kick of conviction in my rear for God to finally get a hold of my heart. We all want good results and we want them quickly, but please... Be patient with yourself. Seek forgiveness when necessary and just pick yourself up and try, try, again. Aren't you thankful God doesn't despise our small beginnings? I know I am!

When The Marriage Bed Becomes a Sick Bed

We've all heard the jokes about how poorly men handle sickness. Cartoons, blogs, and even ladies conference speakers jokingly bemoan the fact that men just can't handle illness the way we ladies can manage being laid up. I get it... those jokes are good for a cheap laugh. Unfortunately, those "lighthearted" jokes aren't really funny because they portray men, and our husbands in particular, as weak and prone to complaints, while setting us up to pridefully proclaim our superior strength. Even when our husbands are truly in pain, we always hold the winning card as we remind them, "Yes, but you never went through childbirth..."

All joking aside, how should a wise wife behave when her husband is ill? Is there a sick bed protocol that brings glory to God? How do we keep the trial of a husband's illness, whether short-term or ongoing, from causing strife and disruption in our marital relationship?

I'm convinced that in order for us to glorify God and bless our husbands through the trial of sickness, we're going to have to eagerly submit two areas of our lives to the direction of the Holy Spirit. Why eagerly? When we are only willing in our submission, it's as though we're holding on to the side of the pool. We'll give this whole "submission to the Holy Spirit" thing a try, but if it doesn't seem to be working out we still have the option to grab that pool wall and do things our way. Eager submission to the Holy Spirit is transformational submission and the only kind of submission that can bring about long term change in our hearts and lives. Eager submission isn't easy because it means sacrificing our perceived right to be in control of our own lives. However, when we embrace the concept of eager, no holds barred submission, we can finally and effectively turn the control of our lives over to the One who can best control it anyway!

Now about those two areas of needed change… The first area is our thought life and how we allow ourselves to consider our husbands. The second area is our actions and how we treat our husbands in their times of illness. As we allow the Holy Spirit to remold and reshape our thoughts and actions, our spouse's illness can become a unique opportunity to grow in our marriage and in our ability to serve lovingly and without hesitation. As always, God can turn what seems to be a burdensome trial into a growth-generating blessing.

Interestingly, throughout the scriptures the mind and the heart are never separated. Although we speak of them in different contexts, according to the Word of God, how the mind thinks… the heart feels and how the heart feels… the mind thinks. They are one and the same entity. That's why it's so important to carefully monitor our thought lives. Garbage spewed into our minds through social media, literature, advice from friends, etc. equals a heart just as full of trash. On the contrary, a mind filled with truth and beauty will produce a heart characterized by that same truth and beauty. Philippians 4:8 clearly lays out this concept for us and is our example to follow as we strive to fill our minds with healthy, Christ-honoring thoughts. It says this:

> *Finally, brethren, whatever is true, whatever is honorable, whatever is right, whatever is pure, whatever is lovely, whatever is of good repute, if there is any excellence and if anything worthy of praise, dwell on these things.*

So what does Philippians 4:8 have to do with our thought lives and how we care for a sick husband? Think about it. It we've filled our minds with the cultural mindset that says our husbands are just big whiner babies and we shouldn't cater to their whims, we'll treat them according to that mindset. If we buy into the idea that "real men just tough it out," we'll expect our husbands to live up to that ideal and we'll secretly, (or not so secretly sometimes) despise them for allowing illness to affect them.

If, however, we have filled our minds with the scriptures, scriptures that speak clearly and frequently of the need to serve one another in love, we will be inclined to care for our husbands tenderly. We'll be prepared, in our hearts, to show compassion and consideration in their time of weakness, rather than judgment and impatience. We'll model for our children, other believers, and nonbelievers alike what it means to "bear one another's burdens." (Galatians 6:2) We will, in fact, in a very real way be the hands and feet of Jesus as we lovingly serve our husbands through their trial of illness.

When our hearts are prayerfully and carefully prepared to love in such a way, it will then be easy to live out the truth found in Matthew 7:12:

"In everything, therefore, treat people the same way you want them to treat you, for this is the Law and the Prophets."

Loving our husbands when they are ill is all about having an other's-oriented focus. Honestly, when we started our married life there wasn't anything I wouldn't do for Steve. (Except make breakfast… obviously anything but that…) However, the first time he was legitimately ill, like so sick he couldn't get out of bed, I had NO idea how to care for him.

Steve and I are completely different when it comes to handling illness! When I'm sick, I tolerate a pat on the head and then I'm thinking, "Goodbye… Close the door behind you and just let me rot here in peace!" I picture myself conversing with Denethor, from The Lord of the Rings, as he says to me, "Go now and die in what way seems best to you!" (Complete with dramatic music and dark shadows) Steve, on the other hand, although he is totally self-sufficient on healthy days, wants to be checked on, hydrated, head patted and basically taken care of by his loving wife.

When I first began to realize what it meant to care for Steve in a way that was meaningful to him, I caught myself frequently thinking, "He just wants me to be his mother." Ever had that thought? It's easy to slip into such a thought pattern and when we do, any service to our husbands will be begrudging at best. Our husbands don't actually want us to be their moms; they just want us to be their wives. You know, those loving, kind, compassionate women they married. They know we're loving, kind, and compassionate because they see us show love, kindness, and compassion to our kids… And our parents… And our friends… And sometimes even strangers…

Ouch!

In Matthew 25:40, Jesus said this:

"The King will answer and say to them, 'Truly I say to you, to the extent that you did it to one of these brothers of Mine, even the least of them, you did it to Me.'"

Good heavens! I don't know about you, but that scripture is absolutely convicting to me. If one of my children is sick, I'll clean their bedroom and put fresh sheets on their bed to help them be more comfortable. If one of my friends is ill, I'll make a meal and deliver it to their home. If someone from church, even someone I don't know well, is in the hospital, I'll go sit with them so they aren't lonely. Why then, is it so stinking hard to do the same for my hard-working husband??

I don't know if it's pride, stubbornness, or a wrong cultural view of men, but for some reason serving a sick husband just doesn't seem to flow from me as naturally as serving others. Matthew 25:40 says that serving "the least of them," is just like serving Jesus. I verbally profess that my husband is my top priority, nowhere near "the least of them" category, but yet, I hesitate to serve him wholeheartedly.

If you're anything like me and you find it easy to lovingly serve others in their times of illness, but not your husband, please allow me to share a few ideas. None of these ideas are earth shattering, but they have helped me to squash my wrong attitudes regarding Steve during his infrequent times of sickness and they've also helped me to realign my heart and actions.

Our first action step is prayer. (Isn't that always the first place we should run?) Obviously, when our husbands are ill we should pray for God to place His healing hand on them. However, our prayers should go much further than just asking God to do His part. Spend time seeking God's direction and conviction to learn how to lovingly serve your husband. Sometimes, for me, that meant asking God to forgive me for my unloving, or just plain lazy attitude toward getting up off of the couch in order to meet my husband's needs. Pray for eyes to see unmet needs and a heart that can serve joyfully. Prayer has the power to change and transform both our attitudes and our actions and God delights to see His women serving Him by serving their spouse!

Secondly, take some time and make a comprehensive list. On that list, record all of the ways your husband has served you during times of illness. If your marriage relationship is anything like mine, you've probably had more "sick in bed" days than your beloved. How did he serve you during those times? How did he extend compassion to you? What actions did he carry out that made you feel loved and cared for throughout your illness?

Steve and I have been married for 32 years. During those 32 years I have been pregnant for approximately 63 months. That's 280 weeks. Or, 1,960 days. (More or less) I can hardly even wrap

Pray for eyes to see unmet needs and a heart that can serve joyfully.

my brain around those numbers! For the majority of those 1,960 days I had some kind of "I just don't feel well," going on. Whether it was the early, interminable days of throwing up, the months of heartburn, or the end of pregnancy sleepless nights, Steve cared for me so tenderly. He cleaned the house, including areas he never would have cleaned except for the fact that he knew it was important to me. He paid for countless restaurant and delivery meals because he recognized that preparing dinner was always during my sickest time of the day. He held my hair back while I vomited. He ran to the store when I thought of some food that seemed like it might just possibly stay down and he never complained when I changed my mind and couldn't eat that same food. He was unfailingly loving, kind, and compassionate toward me in my times of neediness!

When I take the time to remember all of the ways that Steve so carefully and faithfully tended to my needs during the trials of pregnancy, it softens my heart. Those memories spark a desire to serve him in the same way he served me. They remind me that it is a privilege to serve a man who has served me so sweetly.

This idea of making a "memory list" in order to be strengthened in our desire to serve isn't just a feel-good idea. Throughout the Old Testament, Israel was instructed to set up memorials and celebrate feast days for the specific purpose of remembering the goodness of God on their behalf. Those remembrances helped to strengthen God's people to love and serve Him more. In the New Testament, the Apostle Paul recounted to many of the churches his fond memories of their service on his behalf and he reminded them that as he remembered them, he prayed tenderly for their wellbeing. So too, remembering the blessings we've received through our husband's loving service will strengthen us to reciprocate and should prompt prayers of gratitude and thanksgiving.

This final idea will probably seem familiar after reading the earlier chapters, but we can always use the reminder. When it comes to serving our husbands individually and appropriately during their trial of illness, we must each become a careful student of our own unique spouse. Perhaps some of you are lucky and have a husband who, like me, just wants to be left alone while they are sick. (Sorry Steve!) However, after talking with many other wives, I would have to guess that such a husband is not the norm. Therefore, we must each study and observe what acts of service and expressions of compassion are the most meaningful for our own husband. Does he like to have cool drinks brought to the bedside? Would a tidy room make the illness less stressful? Does he want his head rubbed or his feet massaged? Would he feel cared for if you just sat quietly by his bedside and kept him company? Each wife will minister differently to her own husband because God has made each of our husbands uniquely in His image.

Remember when I told you the other squadron wives didn't "applaud" me when I began to prepare Steve his breakfasts? Unfortunately, when other women see you prayerfully and carefully tending to an ill husband, they may not respond with praise and encouragement. That "men are just babies," cultural paradigm is a strong one indeed! That's ok. You can be the first kid on your block to change the way things are done! Unapologetically and with no shame serve your husband and meet his needs. God is aching to bless you and His blessing outweighs any petty criticism you may encounter. Remember that your earthly service to your husband is eternally recognized as service to your Lord.

When we are slow or unwilling to respond to our husband's needs during a time of illness, we are paving the way for misunderstanding and miscommunication. Then, the difficult trial brought on by illness becomes even more challenging. Pray for a soft, compassionate heart toward your husband's needs. Remember fondly his acts of loving kindness toward you. Study and observe how to assist him appropriately and in ways that are significant to him. Most importantly, don't allow a trial brought on by illness to become a wound inflicted by your lack of selfless service and considerate compassion.

Don't Doubt In the Dark What You Know To Be True In the Light

I married the most optimistic man on earth. Steve has always seen the cup as half full. He'll always eat dessert first if he has the option. Even when times are good, he's convinced there's something even better around the corner. To this melancholy, check the block, everything is serious wife of his, that unquenchable optimism has sometimes seemed downright annoying!

But annoying or not, I was always totally content with and somewhat begrudgingly envious of Steve's happy-go-lucky personality. That's why I was so completely blindsided by his four-year bout with depression. In what seemed like the blink of an eye, my light-hearted husband was replaced by a dark, discouraged man I didn't even recognize.

In 2000, we left our home in Pennsylvania for Steve to plant a church in Topsham, Maine. Oh those beginning few years were just a blast! Everyone who came to the church came prepared to grow and serve. We started new ministries, built new relationships, and watched the Holy Spirit move in people's hearts. For my "big idea" guy husband it was the perfect environment and he woke up every day with a song in his heart and a smile on his face.

About year five, things began to change. Just that quickly, the "but we've never done it that way," bug began to infect our church. Suddenly, we weren't eager to welcome visitors and looking for ways to affect our community. Instead, too many members were looking horizontally. They were inspecting one another's lives and choices and finding their fellow believers lacking. The sweet spirit that had characterized our church was being poisoned by "religion," with no eye toward "relationship." I watched my husband begin to wilt.

At the same time, our counseling load was increasing by the day. We were thrilled to see marriages changed as couples interacted with the truths of the scripture. We had begun writing and teaching new marriage and parenting curriculums that were bearing fruit in the lives of folks in our community. That positive fruit was what kept my husband moving forward day by day.

Then it happened. Sin issues within the church leadership caused gossip and strife. Church discipline caused members to turn against other members. The constant weight of counseling, coupled with losing the aid of those who had assisted in the ministry by helping to carry the load of daily church responsibilities, sent my optimistic husband into a downward spiral of deep, dark depression.

Instead of bounding out of bed in the morning, he dragged himself downstairs and forced himself to go to the church. Instead of bubbling over with ideas in his "free" time, he sat silently in his favorite chair, just staring at the wall. Instead of excitedly anticipating the "next great thing around the corner," he dreaded the thought of more of the same old discouragement. He was a shell of the man I had married and I didn't know what to do!

The reality of men dealing with depression is becoming an epidemic problem. I'm not sure if our men are just learning to be more vulnerable and they're finally sharing their feelings, or if the ever-stressful nature of our busy culture is just producing more feelings of depression, but all of the studies show an upward trend in this matter of depression.

Have you been there or are you in the trenches at this moment; are you dealing with a trial brought on by a husband who has lost his hope? If so, please don't feel alone! Depression is one of those hush-hush areas of the church and when someone in our family is experiencing it, too often we feel isolated and unsure of where to turn for help. Well-meaning friends and family members tend to compound the issue by judging the source of the depression, questioning the faith of the depressed person, or labeling depression as a consequence for sin. When the person they're talking about is your husband, their help becomes nothing more than another boulder heaped on your already burdened heart.

Depression, regardless of its cause, is no laughing matter. It isn't a trial that's just magically going to disappear and it demands a special level of love and compassion. Consider how God describes the devastation of depression in Proverbs 18:14

The spirit of a man can endure his sickness, but as for a broken spirit who can bear it?

Who can bear it indeed? Thankfully, God's Word doesn't leave us wondering what becomes of those who are living with a broken

Depression, regardless of its cause, is no laughing matter.

spirit. When it comes to God's tender care of such a person, the answer is found in Psalm 34:18:

The Lord is near to the brokenhearted and saves the crushed in spirit.

It makes me beyond thankful to know that God has His hand on our husbands as they deal with depression. It's a relief to realize that they are safely in His watchful care. But what about us? How can we help our husbands when they are sliding downward on the miry slope of depression? Having walked through four years of dark days, I have a few ideas to share that I'm praying will provide you with some practical tools and a heart full of hope. However, what I'm going to share is in no way definitive. Because of that, I want to encourage you to read, research, and seek help from your Pastor as necessary. If you allow yourself to become isolated and alone as you deal with your husband's depression, trust me, you will only set yourself up to become depressed as well!

The last thing a depressed husband needs to hear is "Just snap out of it!" Although we may not understand exactly what they are feeling, our husbands need us to sympathize with them and not judge them. For some of you who have dealt with depression yourselves, the ability to empathize (or literally feel along with) your husband will help you as you come alongside your husband.

Steve's depression brought about great growth in my prayer life. So often, I couldn't seem to reach him and help him with the dark thoughts. I didn't understand what triggered the darker days and because of that I didn't know how to help him avoid those triggers. Prayer accomplished so many things during that time. First, and foremost, prayer refocused my fearful heart on the God who loved both my husband and me so deeply. Remembering that the depression was a trial already foreseen by God helped me to hold on to hope for the future.

I learned to make my prayers for Steve very specific. Instead of praying that the depression would just go away, I began to pray that Steve would see one obviously God-produced moment of encouragement each day. I prayed that God would bring memories of great joy into Steve's mind. I prayed that we, as his family, would find ways to incorporate thankfulness into our daily actions and conversations. Even if Steve didn't enter into our conversations, the atmosphere of thankfulness in our home helped him to see God in the midst of the darkness.

I found it vitally important to pray with the children about what was going on with their dad. For the older children, the memory of how light-hearted their dad had once been served to remind them of who he actually was as a person. For some of the younger children, however, the only reference they had of their father was as a pastor, and now a deeply unhappy pastor. As we prayed, I reminded them of Paul's thorn in the flesh, (2 Corinthians 12:7) and we asked God to remove the thorn of depression from their dad. We also prayed that if removing the thorn was not God's plan, that regardless, the depression would allow our family the opportunity to glorify God through the trial.

Some husbands just want to be left alone when they are depressed. Other husbands just need their wife to sit silently by their side. NO husband needs a wife to continually quote scripture or point out how happy they should be feeling. To do so is to make yourself a part of the problem, instead of a trusted counselor. For Steve, I discovered that asking him good questions helped him to process and work through some areas of the darkness.

I would encourage you to ask leading questions, rather than specific questions like: "Why are you depressed?" or "What is it going to take to make you feel better?" I don't believe that most of the time our husbands can even accurately answer those types of questions. Better questions would be: "Can you tell me 3 things that encouraged you today?" "Would going for a drive be relaxing?" "It's beautiful out. Would you like to sit outside with me?" You get the idea, questions that aren't pointed or can't be seen as accusatory will help our husbands communicate without causing further distress.

Don't be hurt or take it personally if your husband doesn't respond favorably to your questions or if he doesn't seem to want to spend time with you. Steve told me that in the darkest days, he so despised himself that he couldn't stand to be with anyone. If he needs it, give your husband space to just sit alone and think.

Obviously, you can't force your husband to talk or get help, but you can certainly prepare the fertile soil for him to begin to desire to do those things. The beauty of creation is a wonderful balm for a heart that is mired in darkness. Often, I would ask Steve to join me on a walk. We didn't talk much during those walks, but God's marvelous handiwork ministered peace to his troubled heart.

Every husband is different, but for Steve, keeping our home uncluttered helped him to relax. We noticed, and he actually articulated, that when the house was cluttered, he felt worse. What an easy thing it was for me to keep the house picked up in order to help him cope with the darkness. For the children, it provided a concrete way to come alongside and serve their dad.

Physical issues can compound and sometimes even be the underlying cause of depression. Encourage your husband to get a physical. Even if the results say he is completely physically healthy, it will be a relief to know that his depression isn't coming from some physical ailment. Providing a healthy diet, even when it seems like all he craves is junk food, is one way to care for your husband. Steve found stress-relief in eating, and although I didn't ever tell him NOT to eat what he was craving, I did make sure to provide regular and nutritious meals in between those snacks! Every time he said, "Food is my friend," I would respond with a hug and say, "No, I'm your friend!"

Women are fixers at heart and it is so hard to watch our husbands struggle with discouragement and depression. Unfortunately, this isn't an area we can just fix! It takes time to learn how to appropriately minister to your husband, and even when you do find practical ways to help, it may not change the situation. For a wife committed to living wisely with her husband, the trial of depression builds patience, and faithfulness, and steadfastness, and long-suffering, and compassion. However, without that commitment to wisdom, we can just as easily become impatient, unfaithful, harsh, bitter, and just plain fed up.

I mentioned earlier in this section that if we aren't seeking help for ourselves, and if we aren't clinging to the Word of God, it is so easy to become depressed ourselves. Please, don't let yourself fall into that trap! For four years, Steve struggled with the depression. For the first couple years, I remained the positive, Pollyanna in our marriage. I purposefully chose to look on the bright side, (not the norm for me) and refused to allow negative thoughts to win the day. However, around the end of year three, I began to struggle with my own dark thoughts. I couldn't see the light at the end of the tunnel and quite honestly, I was just tired of the heavy weight and discouraging atmosphere in our home. I unwittingly slipped into the same dark place as my husband.

Up until that point, our home had still functioned fairly normally. However, once both Steve and I were struggling to make it through the days due to our discouragement, the whole family began to suffer. My kids began to show signs of insecurity and everyone chafed under the heavy weight of depression. Not a good place to be! Let me say it again… Please, please, please don't get to that point! Find a friend, or counselor, or pastor who can minister to you as you minister to your husband! Immerse yourself in the scriptures and cling to God's precious promises for you, your husband, and your whole family.

Slowly but surely, God tenderly walked Steve and I both out of the trial of depression. We would ask each other every single day to recount three things that encouraged our hearts. At first, it was just plain hard… Really hard! But day-by-day, it was easier to see encouraging things. Day-by-day we began to wake up with a lighter heart. Day-by-day the darkness slipped away and life was once again hopeful.

I wish I could tell you there was a specific timeline for just how long a husband's depression will last. There just isn't such a timeline and the trial of depression will look different in each husband's life. What I can promise you is this: If you embrace his trial of depression and purpose to glorify God while compassionately loving your husband, you will grow. Your prayer life will grow and your heart of mercy and sympathy toward others will mature.

Steve and I are on the other side of those years of depression now. Although, I must be honest and admit that there are still certain triggers that can send each of us reeling. Thankfully, we've learned to recognize those triggers and we have a deep commitment that we will always point one another toward truth. Sadly, we're learning that at least for us, depression isn't a once and done thing. Darkness is always ready to rear it's ugly head, but once you've walked through the darkness and regained the beauty of the light, the desire to stay in the light is a strong impetus to cling tightly to joy.

Once upon a time, I would have described myself as a person who lacked the gift of mercy. Watching Steve walk through the dark valley of depression and dealing with my own darkness has changed that completely. Remember how I said that God would bring about the good from our trials? It was hard to see that good when my husband was dealing with discouragement and depression, but now, God has begun to give us a glimpse of His bigger purposes.

As Steve and I travel the country teaching marriage and parenting conferences, God has opened a door of unexpected ministry for us. Everywhere we go, God is providing the opportunity for us to meet and pray with dear pastors and their wives. So many of these faithful servants are dealing with just the same type of depression Steve faced while he was a pastor. They feel alone and unable to share their deep hurt with the people to whom they minister. To them, we are a safe haven and a place where they can freely share their hearts. God has graciously brought us through deep waters so that we can minister to others who face the same trials we faced. What a great God we serve!

It's not just pastors that deal with depression, however. Men (and obviously women, as well) from all walks of life can be sucked down into the valley of darkness and depression. No one is immune from the trial of depression, but we can find hope in the midst of the darkness. If you find yourself ministering to your own husband in a trial caused by depression, don't lose heart. Pray consistently and persistently. Minister compassionately. Seek help to carry the burden. And finally, remember that you are not alone in the battle! God loves you, He loves your family, and He will bring good out of a dark, dark trial!

When Sin Rears Its Ugly Head

This last section of the chapter is by far the hardest section for me to write. In fact, I've been putting it off for several days as I contemplated what I would say over and over in my mind. I want to be so careful to be accurate with the scriptures and the heart of God, but I also don't want to inadvertently wound any dear sister dealing with this issue.

What exactly is the issue? This final section is all about dealing with the trials brought on by a husband who is living in sin. Like depression, this is one of those "untalked about" subjects in our churches. Although your friends may have an inkling about what it going on in your home, in most cases, wives tend to protect their husband's reputations by not seeking help.

It's interesting to me just how easy it is for us to share our husband's annoying mistakes. I've been in ladies groups where one story about an inconsiderate husband escalates into an all-out flood of "Can you believe he__________" tales of woe. We share those stories to garner pity. We share those stories to get a laugh. We share those stories to elevate ourselves at our husband's expense. Yes, there are lots of reasons we share our husband's failures, but for some reason, when it comes to sinful behaviors, we clam up.

Don't get me wrong, I'm not saying we should trumpet our husband's sin from the church's steeple, I'm just saying it's interesting where we draw the line. I know for a fact that there are men (and women, too) sitting in the pews each week with an outward appearance of holiness, but an inward life of unconfessed sin. Although their pew mates may be fooled, God sees and knows the hypocrisy of their life. While maintaining such a secret may keep a husband's reputation intact, it causes nothing but harm to his spiritual life.

So, how is a wise wife to handle the knowledge of her husband's sinful choices? I've heard a lot of teaching on this subject, and quite frankly, most of it was what my husband would call, "bad bible!" Scripture, taken out of context, has too often kept wives from helping their husband recognize his sin and seek the help they both need. The bible truly does have some guidelines to help wives as they interact with a husband who has made the choice to walk down a sinful avenue. However, before we look at the action steps laid out in the scriptures, we must first lay some foundational groundwork.

Our foundational groundwork begins with a working definition of sin. Remembering our natural inclination to rationalize our own bad choices, while judging the sins of others, we must be careful to define sin biblically. Although the scriptures never categorize sins and rank them from least to worst, in this chapter we're going to deal with some areas of sin that are particularly devastating to a marriage and potentially dangerous to a wife.

Yes, our husband's may deal with the sin of laziness. (So do we sometimes!) They may gossip at times. (Heavens! If the church began to take gossip seriously we'd have to install Kleenex holders in every pew and Christians would be weeping and crushed by their sin… Hey, maybe that's not such a bad idea!) Although unbiblical and damaging to their personal testimonies and walk with the Lord, gossip is not an area of sin that is particularly dangerous to a wife. A husband who forgets to take out the trash is not sinning; he's just forgetful. A husband who forgets your birthday, ignores Valentine's Day, and misses your special anniversary is not sinning… He's a lot of other things like inconsiderate, thoughtless, and perhaps reckless, but he's not sinning. There are, however, sin areas that must not be ignored and instead, must be dealt with carefully, yet decisively.

The three sin areas we will be addressing are addiction, abusive behavior, and adultery. These three areas, when left unaddressed, are dangerous to a wife and children and can lead to even deeper depths of sin. Often, a sinful appetite in one of these three areas will tempt our husbands to walk down the path of another one of the areas. All three areas strike at the heart of a marriage by destroying trust, cultivating insecurity, and breeding fear.

Any discussion of husbands and their sin appetites seems to lead inevitably to I Peter 3:1-2. Let's take a look at this scripture and then we'll apply it to this trial of dealing with a husband's sin problem.

In the same way, you wives, be submissive to your own husbands so that even if any of them are disobedient to the word, they may be won without a word by the behavior of their wives, as the observe your chaste and respectful behavior.

Think for a moment about all of the different ways you've heard this passage of scripture taught. To begin, often the scripture is taught as an instruction specifically written to wives of unsaved men. Now obviously, men who do not know the Lord are going to be "disobedient to the word," however, I can promise you that saved men can be just as disobedient. Do you know how I can say that so confidently? It's because this saved wife is too often disobedient to the word and I have saved children who choose to be disobedient to the word, often with their saved friends who are making the same unbiblical choices. Do you get it? This scripture is for all wives because every husband has the potential to live unbiblically.

The other thing I've noticed in the teaching of these verses is the unbalanced emphasis on the phrase, "without a word." When this part of the verse becomes the focus of the teaching, it conveys the message that we are to be silent about our husband's sin. I've even had teachers emphatically state that a wife should never point out her husband's sin, but instead should pray for another man to notice and confront him about his sin.

That may sound good, but it certainly isn't biblical! We can't limit our understanding of how we deal with a spouse's sin to one verse. We need to consider the whole counsel of God and when we do so, we'll discover what may at first seem like a contradictory truth. Luke 17:3 states:

"Be on your guard! If your brother sins, rebuke him; and if he repents, forgive him."

We'll come back to that verse later, but for now, please consider how I Peter 3:1 and Luke 17:3 interrelate to one another. In Ephesians 4:15, we are instructed to speak the truth in love. James 5:19-20 provides an even clearer understanding of how we are to approach another believer's sin when it says:

My brothers, if anyone among you wanders from the truth and someone brings him back, let him know that whoever brings back a sinner from his wandering will save his soul from death and will cover a multitude of sins.

No one loves your husband more than you. Therefore, no one has a deeper desire to see him freed from his sin and walking faithfully with Jesus. To remain silent is to desert him to his sin.

Instead of the focus of I Peter 3:1-2 being on a woman's silence, the focus truly should be, as always, on our need to exhibit "chaste and respectful behavior." The dictionary defines the word chaste like this:

Pure in thought and act

In other words, a woman displays her chaste behavior as she deals with her husband respectfully and purely. As she keeps her own sin from making an already difficult situation worse, she can minister truth to her husband.

Without a word doesn't mean being a silent doormat when it comes to your husband's sin. What it does mean is that we must be women who realize that our husbands will never be won over in obedience to the Lord by our onslaught of words. We can't change their minds about their sin by continually quoting scripture or questioning them to see if they've been sinning. It is as they see us faithfully living a walk of obedience that they will be convicted of their sin. Our nagging, harsh, or bitter words will be to no avail. We must call sin, sin, and then entrust our husbands to God.

Why is it so important to verbally acknowledge our husband's sin? Our culture is a culture that hates whistle-blowers. From the time we are tiny children, the admonition to never be a tattletale is deeply imprinted in our minds and hearts. We carry that same paradigm into our adult relationships, but when it comes to dealing with sin, ignoring the issue will only bring about devastating results.

In other words, a woman displays her chaste behavior as she deals with her husband respectfully and purely.

It may seem as though ignoring our husband's sin is a shortcut to ensuring peace in our home, but I promise you that peace will only be short lived. Ultimately, our strongest desire, as believers should be to help other believers recognize their destructive sin and turn in repentance to the Lord. When we refuse to acknowledge our husband's sin, whether out of fear, avoidance, or a misplaced sense of loyalty or submission, we are in fact leaving them to wallow in that very sin. Addressing the sin area brings it out of hiding and is the most loving thing a wife can do.

Gently confronting our husbands about the sin that is entangling them is like turning on the lights in a dark room. Sin festers and breeds in darkness and unexposed sin finds safety in a "lights out" environment. The only reason any of us, including our husbands, sin is because the particular pet sin we have chosen is enjoyable to us. We hold on to sin because the pleasure of the moment is more important than the consequences of that sin. We continue to sin because we have a wrong understanding of exactly how our holy God feels about our sin! John 3:19-20 clearly shows our attitude toward sin and how that sin separates us from God.

"This is the judgment, that the Light has come into the world, and men loved the darkness rather than the Light, for their deeds were evil. For everyone who does evil hates the Light, and does not come to the Light for fear that his deeds will be exposed."

When we lovingly confront our husbands and expose their sin to the light, we are simply acting as God's messengers. As such, we have the beautiful opportunity to help them recognize the devastating consequences of their sin and the powerful forgiveness offered by their Savior.

Let's spend just a few minutes discussing those three sin areas. Again, our husbands will sin in a multitude of other areas (we will too!) but these three areas are the most detrimental, dangerous, and devastating to a marital relationship. The first area is the area of sinful appetites of addiction. Often, when we hear the word, addiction, our first thought is of drug or alcohol abuse. Obviously, a husband who is addicted in one of those two areas is choosing a sinful path, but addiction encompasses so much more. For example, too many men have allowed themselves to dabble in pornography and that dabbling has led to addiction. Ladies, pornography is not acceptable even if "everyone" looks at it!

A somewhat newer, but equally destructive form of addiction is the addiction to video games. I can't begin to count the number of young couples we have counseled that found themselves in a constant state of strife because of the husband's addiction to gaming. Just as alcohol or drugs can become the "must have" of a man's life, gaming can become absolutely irresistible temptation. I've talked with wives who berated their husbands about their gaming, stood in front of the television, and even cut the television cord. Guess what… Their efforts were to no avail because their husbands couldn't recognize the truth of what they were trying to say because of the contentious picture they were presenting by their actions and attitudes. There's a better way, I promise, and we'll get there soon.

Addictive sins breed in secrecy. Husbands who don't come to bed at night, hide their computer screens, or lock themselves away from the rest of the family are often dealing with sins of addiction. Sadly, addictive behavior doesn't ever remain status quo; rather it grows and demands more stimulation to feed the addiction. Ignoring addictive behavior won't make it go away, it will only make it worse.

The second area of sin we need to discuss is abusive sin. Abusive sin is categorized into emotional abuse and physical abuse. This is a tricky area to pin down. I have spoken with women who wanted to define any type of marital strife by using the word, "abuse." Or, if their husband told them NO, they considered it abusive. Ask any woman who is trapped in a truly abusive situation and she'll tell you that those instances are not abuse! True abuse seeks to control and manipulate the one being abused. Emotional abuse will tear down a woman's self-respect. When the abuse is ongoing and continual it can begin to erode a woman's walls of self-preservation. Often, emotionally abused women will, over time, begin to think they deserve the destructive and ugly words that are flung in their direction. Nothing could be further from the truth.

Physical abuse somewhat speaks for itself. It is never, ever, ever appropriate for a husband to strike a wife! (Or vice versa) Hair pulling, slapping, or constraining a wife so that she cannot move is unacceptable behavior in any circumstance. Both emotional and physical abuse can extend beyond the wife to other members of the family, and even if she is only the observer of the abuse, a wife must still deal with that sin biblically and emphatically.

Although the steps I will share later in the chapter for dealing with a sinful husband also apply to wives living with abusive husbands, if you are living with ongoing emotional or physical abuse, you must get help immediately! Do not buy into Satan's lie that you somehow deserve the abuse. If you have been physically struck or subjected to debilitating emotional abuse, pack your bag, grab your children, and find a safe haven. That does not mean your marriage is over, but you must put secure parameters of safety between yourself and your spouse.

The last area of sin is the sin of adultery. Adultery destroys the very foundation of a marriage. What God has put together; adultery tears apart. The sin of adultery has permanent and long lasting consequences. That does not mean that a marriage damaged by adultery cannot be saved. It does not mean that the adulterer cannot be forgiven. However, the serious nature of this particular sin needs to be recognized and dealt with carefully.

Those are the three major areas of sin and they encompass a wide variety of sinful practices. Now, how does a wise wife approach her husband to deal with any of these areas? First, I must encourage you to pray for a heart that is prepared to forgive. Without such a heart attitude, it will be impossible for you to display that pure, respectful attitude discussed in I Peter 3:1-2. As well, it will be impossible for you to truly desire reconciliation if your heart is not prepared to forgive.

Galatians 6:1 makes clear what our attitude is to be as we deal with a fellow Christian's sin. It says this:

> ***Brothers, if anyone is caught in any transgression, you who are spiritual should restore him in a spirit of gentleness. Keep watch on yourself, lest you too be tempted.***

There you have it. We are to be gentle in our confrontation and our goal should be restoration. However, we are also to be wise lest we

> *We are to be gentle in our confrontation and our goal should be restoration.*

be tempted as well. I don't think this is necessarily talking about us being tempted in the same manner as the one we are confronting. For wives, that temptation would most likely rear its ugly head as anger, or bitterness, or a harsh tongue.

The steps involved in confronting a husband regarding his sin are the same steps we should take with any other believer. The goal of the process is restoration, first with God, and then as a couple. These aren't magic steps and they won't necessarily cause change to happen overnight, but as we entrust our husbands to God and courageously, yet kindly, confront their sin, we can trust Him for the results.

The process we're going to examine is a simple "Go To… Go With… Go For," approach for dealing with sin. We begin by Going To our husband. Do you recall the verse out of Luke? It's Luke 17:3:

"Be on your guard! If your brother sins, rebuke him; and if he repents, forgive him."

If your brother, or in this case, your husband, sins… rebuke him. The first step necessary in order to help your husband recognize and repent of his sin is simply to Go To him and point out that sin. This is probably the hardest step in this three-step process. Going to your husband takes courage and it requires remembering the goal. That goal is not to shame your husband, or make your husband feel bad, or "nail him" for his sin. The ultimate goal is to see a sinner restored to Christ. When we can remember the goal, we can lovingly say what oftentimes is a really harsh truth: "You are in sin."

Although bringing rebuke into our husband's life seems like a harsh action, the Ellicott's Commentary for English Readers sheds some beautiful light on this word "rebuke." Ellicott says this regarding Luke 17:3:

When they (the disciples) saw a conspicuous instance of worldliness or other evil, they did as we so often do-they condemned, but did not rebuke. In practice, as Jesus taught them by example as by precept, open friendly reproof, aiming at restoration, is the truest path to forgiveness.

Rebuke, then, isn't condemnation and it isn't meant to be harsh or hurtful. Instead, it is a loving action meant to precipitate restoration and forgiveness.

This step in the process is not a do-over-and-over-again step. We are to go to our brother, (husband) rebuke him, and then wait for the results. To go back and revisit the conversation over and over is to drown him with our words, while silencing our message.

Philippians chapter four is one of my favorite chapters in the Bible. In verses 1-3 of chapter four, Paul is discussing two women in the church who were causing disruption because they couldn't live peaceably with one another. Paul instructs an unknown "brethren" to go help those women as they learned to "live in harmony in the Lord." Paul, himself, couldn't get to them, but he sent someone else to Go To them, in order to help them to forsake their strife and embrace biblical living.

As we consider Luke 17:3, we see one possible outcome of confronting our husband. He may repent! Honestly, sometimes the simple action of pointing out a brother's sin is the very impetus they need in order to desire to repent and be done with their sin. That's why it is so important to begin this process prayed up and prepared to forgive. If our husband repents and we refuse to forgive… We're the ones that are then in sin!

What, however, if our husbands don't repent? What if we carefully and respectfully point out their sin and they just refuse to acknowledge that sin? What then? If our husbands refuse to repent, the next step is to offer to Go With them to seek help. This second step is so important because it reminds our husbands that they are not alone in their battle against sin. We are their greatest allies and we're willing to stand beside them in the battle. Encourage your husband to seek the counsel of your Pastor or another godly counselor. Make yourself available to work around his schedule in order to make such a meeting happen. You don't have to rehash your earlier conversation about his sin! Trust me, he'll remember what you talked about and understand why you want him to seek counsel.

If he agrees to accompany you to counseling… Praise God! As you join him in his counseling time allow him to do the talking. You should quietly spend that time beseeching the Lord on his behalf. Verbalize to your husband just how thankful you are that he is willing to deal with the issue at hand and affirm his positive steps… even if they seem like baby steps!

Sometimes, sadly, a husband not only refuses to acknowledge his sin, but he also refuses to get help. Then, a wife will need to move to step 3. At this point, she will have to Go For him. Going For him is only appropriate if you go to the right person! Going For your husband Does Not mean you have the freedom to tell all of your girlfriends about his sin. It does not release you to run to your parents and tell them all of your husband's issues. The correct place to go is to your Pastor. Your Pastor will be able to help you and begin the process of reaching out to your husband. Like you, his goal will be to see your husband restored to Christ.

If you go to the wrong counselors, you will receive bad counsel! It's so easy for our girlfriends (online or in person) to encourage us to just walk away. When we're discouraged by a lack of repentance and restoration, that solution can seem so easy! Be self-disciplined and only seek out help from a pastor or counselor.

God hates divorce! (Malachi 2:16) However, if a husband refuses to repent of his sin and if that sin becomes dangerous for a wife, at times, separation may be the answer. Temporarily extricating yourself from a harmful situation may be the very means God uses to get your husband's attention. Separation is never to be punitive or a knee jerk reaction, but if you are in danger or if your husband refuses to recognize his sin, it may be the only solution. Leave if you must, but earnestly pray and implore the Lord to reach the heart of your husband and restore your marriage.

Dealing with the trial of a husband ensnared by sin is probably the most difficult trial a woman can face. At such a time, it's even more important than usual to be immersed in the Word of God and surrounded by faithful prayer warriors. Even when your prayer warriors don't know the exact details concerning your husband's sin, they can still intercede on your behalf and provide the prayer support you need to stay strong in the battle. Regardless of your husband's behavior, prove yourself to be a wise wife by your chaste and respectful behavior. Refuse to ignore sin, but choose to love the sinner. Allow God to do mighty things on your behalf and never lose heart in the battle.

Galatians 6:9 provides the hope we need as we continue to entrust ourselves to God. It says:

Allow God to do mighty things on your behalf and never lose hope in the battle!

And let us not lose heart in doing good, for in due time we shall reap if we do not grow weary.

I can't promise you that your husband will come to repentance. That decision is between him and God. What I can promise you is exactly what God promises... You will reap if you don't grow weary! And we know that whatever we reap from God will be a priceless treasure indeed!

WHAT THE HECK? PART 3

IT'S IN THE DNA

This last section of "What the Heck" topics is somewhat a mishmash, a compilation of various circumstances of life and how they highlight the differences between men and women. Although we'll never change our men and we may never truly understand them, learning to laugh at our differences will clear the air and help us to "lighten up!"

Perhaps nothing highlights the difference between Steve and I as much as how we handle the inhabitants of this crazy household. As I've said before, we have eight children, four boys and four girls. Steve loves the noisiness of those boys. He revels in it. In fact, sometimes he's the instigator of the noise. I, on the other hand, tolerate the noise, and the wrestling, and the farts, and the spitting off of the porch to see whose spit goes the farthest. Although I'm somewhat "noiseaphobic" I can handle it without losing my mind… At least most of the time.

The girls are a different story. For many years, we had our four girls and two extra young women living in the house. In total, we had six girls 13 through 25 living under the same roof. Six girls who stole each other's clothes. Six girls who braided each other's hair. Six girls who could go from cuddling in a giant pile on the couch to not speaking to each other in less than 30 seconds. You get it… Six normal females. Their shenanigans didn't faze me at all. I'm a girl; I get it! For the most part, all of their chatter and noise was much like a fly buzzing in my ear; annoying but easily ignored.

*Just a side note here: That whole fly thing is a major difference between my beloved and me. There I'll be, blissfully sleeping after hours of wakefulness because I've been overthinking my life, when "Bang!" On come the lights. My dearest darling will whisper (as though the fly can hear him) "There's a fly in here and we're never going to be able to sleep until I kill it!" Correction: you're never going to be able to sleep until you kill it… I was sleeping just fine, thank you!

Back to the girls… While their noise, and upheaval, and drama didn't bother me in the least, it got on Steve's very last nerve. One night he took them all into the family room and sat them down and announced that the bickering and making up was OVER! They were sisters and they were going to live like sisters! I didn't have the heart to tell him that actually… they already were living like sisters.

After that, occasionally I'd come out on the porch to a strange male spectacle. There they'd be, all of my men from the oldest to the youngest. When I'd ask what they were doing, one of them would say, "Dad brought us out here to scratch and spit and remember we're men." I guess Steve was afraid all that "femaleness" was going to rub off on his boys! Men just aren't equipped to deal with that much drama for an extended period of time!

Men's powers of observation are another conundrum in my mind. Remember how I said they never miss a scratch or dent on their car? They can tell exactly how and when one of their precious tools was used? How then, can they NEVER find the jar of peanut butter in the pantry… on the shelf… in front of their nose… right where I said it would be!! This, ladies is a question for the ages. Don't try to figure it out… Your brain will simply explode!

Finally, let's talk about men and context. Men, as we know, are always hungry. It's just part of who they are and they can eat amazing quantities of food regardless of the time of day, **and** regardless of the appropriateness of the situation.

When I was expecting my first baby, I had a friend that was due to deliver just a few weeks before my due date. This friend was the most organized woman I'd ever met and she had her birth plan down pat. What she didn't plan on was an extremely LONG labor.

At about the 22-hour point of her labor, Judy finally began to push. There she was with her sweet husband leaning over, right in her face, giving her coaching and encouragement. However, he was leaning over, right in her face, chewing on the beef jerky he had conveniently stowed in his pocket. Judy was such a sweet woman that she didn't complain… to him. To us, though, she tearfully shared the repulsive smell of that nasty beef jerky and how much she just wanted to smack her husband!

I shared that story with Steve and let him know that as far as I was concerned, beef jerky was off-limits in my labor room. Well, he didn't eat any beef jerky…

Three weeks later, I was in labor. I, too, didn't expect the LONG labor that it would take for little Katie to make her entrance into the world. I went for 20 hours with no food. Finally, the kind nurse brought me a tiny cup of Jell-O to give me some strength to keep laboring. You can see it coming can't you?… Steve took a bite of my Jell-O! MY Jell-O!! To this day, he still can't figure out why I reacted so violently to that stolen spoonful of green, jiggly goodness. He's a man and men get hungry! He's lucky I didn't bite him…

Men. Just think what the world would be like if God had allowed one of us women to do all the creating! I don't know about you, but I'm glad for the differences. And on those days that I'm not feeling so glad, I know just what to say:

WHAT THE HECK?

CHAPTER TEN

PUSHING THE RESET BUTTON

"We cannot embrace God's forgiveness if we are so busy clinging to past wounds and nursing old grudges."
T.D. Jakes

Can I just tell you how hard it has been writing this book? As I shared in the beginning of the book, I'll only write about those areas in which God has already been working in my life. Well... I promise you... I've never experienced as much "God-meddling" as I have during the process of preparing and writing this book! Even in those areas that I would have said were fairly under control, God rattled my cage and showed me parts of my heart that I would have preferred to keep under wraps.

Which means that Steve and I have had ample opportunity to work on LOTS of areas of our communication and relationship. How splendid for us! ... But that's the goal. I never want to write anything that isn't as useful for me as it is for you. I have to be honest though, I'm glad we're getting close to the last chapter because quite frankly all of this marital remodeling has been exhausting!

This chapter is really all about what we do when we bump into those areas of marital remodeling and reconstruction. What do we do as a wise wife with unresolved issues, knee-jerk reactions that caused hurt feelings, or words spoken in haste that have caused distance and disharmony? Are we destined to remain in conflict? Should we just allow time and space to take care of the issues? Or, does God have a better way. As always… He does!

Is It Even Worth It To Change?

As we begin to dig into the subject of restoring those areas that need some TLC, we have to begin the discussion by talking about why we would even choose to change. Why do we even want to stir up the status quo? As believers, not even as wives at the moment, just believers in the Lord Jesus Christ, our lives need to be all about change. To remain static as a Christian is to commit spiritual suicide. We are always to be about growing and changing to be more conformed to the image of Jesus Christ.

Where did I come up with that? Well, let's find out together. We're going to spend quite a bit of our time in this chapter looking in the book of Ephesians and we'll start there now. Two passages in Ephesians chapter four are particularly pertinent as we talk about our need to grow and change. The Apostle Paul begins our conversation in Ephesians 4:15-16.

(Paul) but speaking the truth in love, we are to grow up in all aspects into Him, who is the head, even Christ, from whom the whole body, being fitted and held together by that which every joint supplies, according to the proper working of each individual part, causes the growth of the body for the building up of itself in love.

In other words there is no question about it, we are to grow up and strive to look more like Jesus. Whether it's how He acts, how He prioritizes His time, how He relates to people, or how He serves and prays, we are to look more like Him each day.

But Paul didn't end his teaching there. Instead he goes on to instruct us exactly how to go about learning to look more like Jesus. As a good teacher, he didn't just impart the need and the theory, but he went on to give practical instruction and application. In Ephesians 4, verses 20 through 24, Paul communicates the important "put-off/put-on" principle we must live by if we are to embrace biblical change and transformation.

But you did not learn Christ in this way, if indeed you have heard Him and have been taught in Him, just as truth is in Jesus, that, in reference to your former manner of life, you lay aside the old self, which is being corrupted in accordance with the lusts of deceit, and that you be renewed in the spirit of you mind, and put on the new self, which in the likeness of God has been created in righteousness and holiness of the truth.

Putting-off and Putting-On

The put-off/put-on principle tells us that we can't simply hope for Christ-honoring change to occur in our lives. Rather, we must put-off those old sinful habit patterns and worldly appetites that cause us to choose unrighteous paths and instead embrace biblical and Christlike models of proactive living. According to Ephesians 4, such a change in our direction of thinking and acting can only occur as we are renewed in our minds. In other words, as we allow the Word of God to transform us and as we seek biblical input through the preached Word, prayer, fellowship and accountability with other like-minded believers, we will gain the wisdom we need to put-off the old and eagerly put-on the new.

What does this look like in the realm of our marital relationship? I believe that when it comes to growing and changing to look more like Christ and then putting-off old practices in order to embrace new marital practices, the first step is to humble ourselves and ask the Lord to reveal any unbiblical patterns of living that we have allowed to become our model for life. The wise wife will truly desire to change in order to magnify Christ through her marriage and change can only happen if we recognize the need for transformation.

As the Lord begins to open your eyes to areas of needed change, may I encourage you to bring your husband into the conversation? Sometimes it is intimidating to ask our husbands how they think we should grow and change. Do you know why it's so intimidating? It's intimidating because they might actually see some areas that need to be transformed in our lives! I wish I could tell you that every time I've asked Steve if there are any areas of needed growth in my life he's replied, "Absolutely not!" but that just wouldn't be the truth. Steve sees me and knows me better than anyone else in this world. He sees me on my good days, my bad

The wise wife will truly desire to change in order to magnify Christ through her marriage and change can only happen if we recognize the need for transformation.

days, my flat-hair days, my "you're not the boss of me days," and everything in between. If anyone knows where I'm not bringing glory to God… It's him.

There are a few ways we can respond when our husbands point out needful areas of change in our lives. Trust me, I've done all of these! The first way we can respond is to ignore what they're telling us. After all… Who does he think he is? This response does nothing for our spiritual life and even less for our marriage. If you want to train your husband to simply keep his nose out of your business and be uninterested and uninvolved in your spiritual growth, just ignore everything he says to you.

The second way we can respond is to argue with him and tell him that he's wrong. Or, my personal favorite, tell him that he's "judging me." Nothing will cause a man to initially fight back, but then retreat and avoid you, like a woman who asks for his input and then makes him pay for whatever he says.

A third and very effective way to avoid growing and changing is to point out your husband's own failures in the very area in which he's trying to encourage you to grow. If you can divert the attention to his own lack of spiritual living, or better yet blame your weaknesses on him, you can circumvent the need to take ownership for your own spiritual life, while all the while pointing out his flaws and failures.

I'm ashamed of how often I still resort to one of these unbiblical and unattractive methods of communication. God has a simple method to help us hear and internalize those changes our husbands have the courage to share with us. His method is found in James 1:19.

This you know my beloved brethren. But let everyone be quick to hear, slow to speak, and slow to anger.

If we really want to live lives that are characterized by wisdom and biblical change we must be quick to hear. Hearing doesn't just mean technically listening, but rather it indicates an ear that has been fine-tuned by a heart that is eager to be transformed. Then, we must be slow to speak. So often as our husbands try to lovingly challenge us in some area of our marriages or personal lives, we are already formulating our rebuttal and the Holy Spirit has no opportunity to bring conviction into our hearts. Finally, we need to temper our first response. When we allow our first response to be anger, rather than thoughtful and prayerful contemplation of what's been shared, we will never be able to make those changes that will transform our lives and marriages, and ultimately bring glory to God.

With this verse in mind, may I share a fourth way that we can receive input from our husbands. I believe this fourth way is a way that will help us hear, will show our husbands respect, and will best prepare the rocky ground of our hearts to be fertile soil prepared to embrace seeds of growth and change. The fourth way is simply this: when our husbands offer their counsel we can choose to say, "Thank you."

Thank you is so powerful! It communicates a willingness to listen and an appreciation for a husband who is willing to interconnect with us. Thank you reminds us to be humble and teachable. Thank you is the first step to embracing biblical change.

The Bible Tells Me So

Sometimes change is simple. Sometimes it's nothing more than fine-tuning some area of our marriage or personal life in order to make life run more smoothly. Sometimes, it's just a change our husbands think will make our marriage more intimate; it isn't that we've been choosing a wrong path, it's just a suggestion to try a ne, and perhaps more productive path.

However, many times when we're confronted with the need to change, whether that confrontation comes through what we've discovered in our time spent in the Word, constructive input from our husband, or far too often, conflict and disagreement, the next course of action needs to be repentance, seeking forgiveness, and finally, carrying out meaningful acts of restoration. When this is the case, all three of these actions need to be carried out with both God and our husband.

If you can learn to repent, seek forgiveness, and restore quickly, your marriage will be strengthened and solidified on a rock-solid foundation. Time, space, and apology do not bring about the same resolution to strife. All they do is delay dealing with the issue at hand and often they make the entire situation worse. Those are the times we find ourselves in a confrontational discussion and we can't even figure out how we got there!

When we don't deal with strife according to the biblical model of repentance, seeking forgiveness, and initiating restoration we cause infection in the marriage relationship. I think of it this way: Using any means other than the biblical means of resolving conflict is like putting a Band-Aid on an open and gaping wound. Imagine your spouse came to you with an injury from working outside. His flesh was torn and there were dirt and wood splinters in the wound. Next, imagine that all you did was pull a Band-Aid out of the medicine cabinet and place it over the torn flesh without ever cleaning out the wound. What would happen next? In a few days, when you pulled that bandage off the wound would be just as ugly, and in fact it would probably be red and filled with the puss of infection. It certainly led and you would have made a minor injury ›lesome.

…unds in our marriage react just like that physical injury. When we simply try to cover over the issue at hand by allowing time, space, or an easy apology to act as a Band-Aid, we are in effect masking an open wound. When we inadvertently rip off the bandage later during another time of miscommunication or strife, the wound will still be just as raw. Sometimes, we'll be confused because we assumed that the issue had been taken care of because it seemed to have disappeared from the conversation. However, without the healing ointments of repentance, forgiveness, and restoration all that has happened is that the original wound has been left to fester.

I know for some of you this teaching is old hat. You've been a Christian for years and you already know that you need to seek forgiveness when you've wronged your spouse. However, this teaching is so critical and I think as Christian wives we have so misused or ignored its importance that I'm going to spend some time exploring just how it works. Please bear with me and may I encourage you to read this chapter thoroughly, even if it seems like old news. We can all use the reminder to restore appropriately and thoroughly and perhaps, just perhaps, we need our memories jogged to help us live more biblically.

The Starting Line

Repentance is only possible when we recognize that we have done something wrong or chosen a way of living that is not honoring to God. Simply defined, repentance basically means to change our mind about something and then to literally walk in a different direction. In other words, we realize that a habit pattern or way of living is unbiblical and we make a 180-degree turn to begin living and acting in the opposite way. Picture walking down the road toward a steep cliff and then realizing you are about to plunge to your death, so you quickly turn around and walk the other way.

I think sometimes we don't pursue repentance in our relationship with our husbands because we think repentance is only reserved for those BIG issues that might have long-lasting consequences for our marriages. Nothing could be further from the truth and I think this understanding will be easier to embrace if we take a quick look at how the bible describes anger and the need to get right with one another.

The key verse regarding anger in our marriage relationship is found in Ephesians 4:26.

> *Be angry and yet do not sin; do not*
> *let the sun go down on your anger.*

Read carefully, this verse does not prohibit anger… It prohibits sinful anger. There is a type of righteous anger like that modeled by Jesus in Matthew 21:12-13, and again in John 2:14-17. However, be careful dear friends! It's so easy and awfully tempting to label our own anger as "righteous" anger. Again, Jeremiah 17:9 reminds us that our hearts are desperately wicked and can fool even us. Part of the reality of our fallen nature is the desire to rationalize our own sinful anger, and then judge the anger of others, and especially our spouse. Ask yourself hard questions and don't cut yourself a break in this area; instead prayerfully allow God's Word to be your mirror and discern carefully what is and isn't "righteous" anger.

This is one of those verses that as my husband says, "Will really preach!" Generally speaking, I've heard this verse applied to indicate that if you and your spouse have blown it with each other, don't go to sleep until you've resolved the issue. In other words, "no sleeping if you're fuming!" Although that's a great application as a starting point, I think it's an incomplete understanding of the scripture.

In Ephesians 4:26, the word anger (or angry) is used twice. Both times the word is used it originates from the same Greek root word and thus indicates the same meaning. Anger (or angry) can be defined three different ways in the Greek language and the definition radically changes the meaning of the verse.

The first definition of the word anger (or angry) is the Greek word Perigismos. Perigismos is defined as mild irritation. Steve always says it reminds him of mothers with toddlers. You know how it is… after being touched, thrown up on, argued with, and disobeyed all day you're just mildly irritated with everyone and everything. This mild irritation is an insidious thing. Couples who have allowed issue after issue to go unresolved will often not even understand how much the level of perigismos has escalated in their marriage. They just walk around all the time with unresolved anger and they don't even realize it anymore. If you've ever gone out on a double date with one of these couples you'll have no problem recognizing the level of perigismos in their relationship. All evening they'll just snipe at one another and bicker, bicker, bicker!

The second type of anger in the Greek language is Orge. Orge is defined as righteous indignation. When your spouse has assigned a motive to your behavior (i.e. "You did that because you're just lazy") you feel that type of righteous indignation. When someone cuts you off in traffic or interrupts you when you're speaking, it's that same type of righteous anger.

The final definition for the word anger (or angry) is found in the Greek word Thumos. Thumos is explosive anger. It's the type of anger that is seen in a spouse who yells, or curses, or throws things. This anger, when left unattended, can lead to physical or emotional abuse or injury. You can't miss thumos because it's loud and ugly.

I'm fairly confident that we would all agree that if our actions, attitudes, or words have caused thumos in our relationship, we need to repent. In other words, if things are getting ugly we'll try to make them right. However, the word used to define anger in Ephesians 4:26 isn't the word thumos and it isn't the word orge, either. Rather, it is the word perigimos or mild irritation.

Does this change your understanding of when the need to repent, seek forgiveness, and restore with one another really is? It isn't when things have escalated to ugly and you are, in some sense, dragged kicking and screaming to repentance. No, it's when you realize that your actions have caused the mildest irritation in your relationship with your husband. If we're quick to get right with each other when we're in that first level of mild irritation, we'll never end up in the ugly place of explosive anger.

Repentance, then, is what starts us down the road to biblical restoration and the hopeful outcome of change and growth. However, repentance alone won't heal the wounds caused by our poor choices.

Repentance, then, is what starts us down the road to biblical restoration and the hopeful outcome of change and growth.

No, once we've "changed our mind" about the direction we were headed, we must seek forgiveness in a meaningful way.

Changing Direction Isn't Enough

Seeking forgiveness begins with God. Ultimately, all of our poor choices and sinful habits are an offense against a holy God. Therefore, we must ask His forgiveness and we can do so knowing that He will always be faithful and just and He will always forgive us. (I John 1:9) But we can't just stop there. Seeking forgiveness from the Lord is step one and sometimes it doesn't seem that hard to do. Step two, however, is seeking forgiveness from our husbands and that requires swallowing our pride, naming our offense, and humbly asking our husband to forgive us.

After seeking forgiveness, (Whew, glad that's over with!) we must find ways to restore the brokenness of our relationship with our husband. Offenses against one another cause distance and destruction. Forgiveness, when coupled with restoration can bridge the distance and cause healing where once there was infection. Sometimes a simple hug may be all the restoration that is needed to make things right again, but a wise wife will take whatever steps are necessary in order to make sure that there is no room for bitterness or continued hurt in her relationship with her husband.

Biblical repentance, forgiveness, and restoration are really God's reset button. Obviously, they are tools that are essential for both members of the marriage, but you can only take responsibility for your use of the tools. Whether your husband practices biblical restoration in your marriage is completely between him and God. You, however, are accountable for how masterfully you wield the tools God has provided for you.

"I'm sorry. Will you please forgive me?" should be a frequent part of your conversation. Honestly, the longer Steve and I are married the more often it seems that we are seeking forgiveness from one another. This is another expression (like thank you) that we can just be so stingy about using. Seeking forgiveness isn't the most we can do in our relationship… it's the least! If you struggle to seek forgiveness, I would direct you to the gospels. The more time you spend dwelling on the unbelievably generous way in which Jesus forgave you in order to have a restored relationship with you, the quicker you will be to seek forgiveness from your husband in order to experience that oneness of restored relationship with him.

Here's What It Looks Like!

Okay, let me make it really practical by giving you an example from my own marriage. I promised I'd be vulnerable and transparent and hopefully as you see what this looks like "in real life" you'll grasp the significance of biblical restoration for your own marriage.

For years, I struggled not to be controlling when it came to "helping" Steve make decisions. Remember we discussed in Chapter 3 how easy it is for us to want to be our husband's personal Holy Spirit or that super hero (complete with cape) who rushes in to save the day. I wasn't making that stuff up! I lived that paradigm for way too many years. It wasn't that I intentionally purposed to disrespect Steve by questioning each and every one of his decisions… every single time he had a decision to make… it was just, well… I thought I knew better than him!

After years of my disrespectful nagging and the subsequent "heated fellowship" we stumbled into over and over again, God began to get my attention. As I studied the Word more deeply I discovered that the important role I thought I'd been filling wasn't really my role at all. I began to recognize that all of the strife we were encountering wasn't because Steve was stubbornly unwilling to bow to my "superior knowledge," but it actually originated in my prideful, haughty attitude. It was absolutely time for me to "put-off" my controlling, nagging nature and "put-on" a respectful, honoring attitude, in order to effectively communicate to Steve that I trusted him and his ability to make good decisions for our family.

Once I realized this truth, I was faced with only one choice. I needed to make it right with Steve. We were well beyond the point of me ignoring the problem, arguing about the issue, or pointing the finger of blame back at Him. This was my "bad" and I needed to own it and change my mind about how I was living with my husband. In other words, I needed to repent!

After purposing in my heart and before God to change my sinful and controlling attitude toward my husband, I sought forgiveness from the Lord. Then, I went to Steve. It would have been so easy to just try to do better and hope that he'd forget how disrespectful I'd been, (I promise, that was a HUGE temptation) but I knew in my heart the only biblical action I could take was to seek forgiveness.

Now, if I ran the world, when you asked for forgiveness that would be the end of the discussion. If I had my choice, our husbands would just smile, nod, and say it's all-good! Unfortunately, so far I haven't been chosen as the Ruler of the World. Sometimes, I behave just like my children. When I have to confront them or bring correction in some area of their behavior, their first response is always "I know! I know!" Just because they say that they know doesn't mean that I stop talking! I need them not to simply "know," but to "understand" the issue we're discussing. Part of seeking forgiveness means humbly listening as our husbands share how our actions have affected them. ("I swear… I already know!) If I didn't already know, I knew after he was done!

The final step was restoring with Steve. I assured him that I would strive to change my attitude and actions toward him. I wish I could have confidently told him it would never happen again, but old habits sometimes die hard. Mark Twain actually said, "Habits can't be kicked out the door; they must be coaxed down the stairs one step at a time." I think maybe Mark Twain had heard about me when he came up with that quote! I told Steve how I had come to realize the need to change and the biblical choices I wanted to make in order to treat him and our relationship differently. Thankfully, I have a husband who is quick to forgive and who chooses to hope the best for me.

With God, All Things Can Be Made New

When we do things God's way the resolution is always so sweet. Do I ever still try to control Steve's decisions? Yep, sometimes I do. However, I've changed the characterization of my life. If you asked him now, he would say that I'm characterized by asking good questions, listening carefully, and offering well thought out counsel, but only as he requests it.

Writing this book has certainly brought to the surface some areas of much needed change. Now the onus is on me to take the

> *When we do things God's way the resolution is always so sweet.*

biblical steps to not only make the changes, but also repair the damage done by my previously disrespectful and poor choices. How about you? Is there anything you need to get right with your husband? I implore you to do it God's way! Don't try to put an unbiblical Band-Aid on the wound. Change your mind about your choices through repentance. Seek forgiveness from God and your husband. Find meaningful avenues of restoration that will rebuild and strengthen your marriage. God is all about helping us as we seek to put-off our old behaviors and put-on new and Christ-honoring actions and if God is for us… who can be against us!

CHAPTER ELEVEN

WRAPPING THINGS UP

"The book doesn't end when you finish writing it."
Claire Tomalin

It's time to wrap things up. Quite honestly, I'm sure there are umpteen more areas of respect, honor, and marriage building we could tackle, but we've got plenty to get us started! I know there's been A Lot in the last nine chapters, but dear sisters, "Let us not lose heart in doing good, for in due time we will reap if we do not grow weary." (Galatians 6:9)

Remember, your marriage and growing and changing in your role as a wife in order to bring glory to the Lord and joy to your marital relationship isn't a sprint! It's a slow and steady marathon that needs to be marked by solid measurable growth. God doesn't ever point out all of our areas of weakness and say, "Get it fixed and do it now!" No, He is so patient with us. He gently shows us areas of needed growth and then strengthens us to make the changes we so desperately need to make. And aren't you glad! If God dealt with me in every area and in every single moment of the day, I wouldn't have the courage to get out of bed in the morning. I can tell you from my own walk with Him, there is no kinder or more patient

Lover of my Soul than Jesus and because of that I long to "put-off" the old Megan and "put-on" the new Megan simply because I love Him so much!

I hope you end these chapters hopeful. I know that anytime we interact with the scriptures and biblical principles we're going to be confronted with the need to change, but please don't let those changes frighten you! Your marriage is worth it! Change, simply for the purpose of changing, is fruitless. However, change with the end goal of magnifying our Lord and cultivating our marriage is worth every bit of effort we expend.

Those two reasons are really the ONLY reasons that will keep you moving forward and looking upward. I could exhort you to change because it will just make life easier. Or, I could try to scare you into making biblical change by sharing the statistics. They're out there and they're scary… The latest polling numbers show that the Christian divorce rate is holding steady at 26%, Just Like The Rest of The World! Although those statistics might bring about some short-term motivation, and although easier days is a tempting thought, those things will never change the attitude of our hearts and they'll never give us the strength we need to "keep on keeping on" when the days are hard and the trials seem endless. When well-meaning friends and family paint a rosy picture of life away from your present circumstances those short-term motivators just won't cut it!

So why change? We change because God loves us and we love Him. We change because we want to please Him by honoring and respecting our husbands in order to live blamelessly before Him. We change because we trust God and He gives us hope for marriages that are beautiful, sweet, loving, and fulfilling. We change because we truly desire to be wise wives who can use their marriages to show Jesus Christ to a watching world.

I'm praying for you, dear sisters! (And you should pray for me too… I'm sure that's pretty obvious by now.) Regardless of how your husband responds to your Christ-honoring changes, regardless of how your sisters or best friends chide you for focusing on yourself, instead of demanding change from him, regardless of how often you feel like a little fish swimming upstream in a giant river, remember that God is aching to bless your obedience and pleasing Him is the greatest blessing of all!

BONUS CHAPTER

I don't know if you've realized this, but most men have rules (spoken and unspoken) for life. While my rules are fairly simple:

1. Always be where you say you are when you say you're there.
2. Make good choices.
3. Always, and I mean Every.Single.Time. Call your mother!

Steve's rules are much more complicated and well thought out. Here for your reading enjoyment are Steve Scheibner's rules for life for men. The italicized sections are my "helpful" commentary as needed.

1. You don't have to like it; you just have to do it. *By far the most repeated rule in our house!*
2. Make the females in your life happy. *My favorite rule… Obviously!*
3. If you're on time, you're five minutes late. *His military background is showing on this one.*
4. Don't step on the rattlesnake. *The rattlesnake is what my husband becomes when he's asleep. This rule eliminates unnecessary middle of the night visits from children, but when there is an emergency guess whom they wake up!*

5. Don't screw the pooch. *I'm not sure as a woman that I can even understand this one. Basically, I think it means that when you have a good thing be careful not to mess it up!*
6. Nothing good happens after midnight. *Funny.... He didn't live by this rule while we were dating...*
7. It's never the crime; it's the cover-up that gets you. *All of our kids have learned this one from hard experience. Don't you wish if one child learned a lesson the others could just learn it through osmosis?*
8. Be motivated by the love of virtue, not the fear of punishment. *He teaches it and lives it!*
9. Be submitted to the authority of God's Word. *He taught me this one way back when we first met and it's been the cornerstone of everything he's taught our family.*
10. Be an eager participant in your own spiritual growth. *Eager... not just willing!*
11. Eagerly embrace radical transformation. *Even if it means moving...starting a church... opening our home...*
12. Always elevate virtues above feelings. *Sometimes this one is so hard because I just don't feel like it!*
13. Make God look great. *Kind of all-inclusive.*
14. Train to be a blessing to others. *And might I add... especially your mother!*
15. Drive fast and take chances. *I hate, hate, and hate this one! Sometimes I think they take this more seriously than my "make good choices" rule!*
16. When it comes to math... just follow your heart. *Can you even believe he made this rule? I'm pretty sure a couple of my boys followed this one on their SATs!*

17. A man wears a watch and a belt. *Trust me, all of my daughters tell their young men this rule before the young man ever comes over to meet my husband!*
18. Never go for either/or when you can go for both/and. *This rule might explain my expanding waistline.*
19. Don't be "That Guy." *I can't even...*
20. Don't cash in all of your tickets at once. *In other words... don't blow it!*

There you have it! Honestly, the differences in the way he and I think are enormous, but that's part of the beauty of our marriage. When you learn to love your differences and laugh about the absurdities that those differences cause, you'll be well on your way to becoming the wise wife God designed you to be. May God bless you on the journey!

Blessings,

Megan

CHAPTER-BY-CHAPTER SCRIPTURES

(For all those times you're wondering, "What was that verse she mentioned…?")

Introduction

Proverbs 31:30

Charm is deceitful and beauty is vain, But a woman who fears the LORD, she shall be praised.

Proverbs 4:7

"The beginning of wisdom is: Acquire wisdom; and with all your acquiring, get understanding.

It's Not About the Wedding… It's About the Marriage

Psyched you out! There are no verses in this chapter!

Men and Women: There Really Is a Difference

I Corinthians 11:3

But I want you to understand that Christ is the head of every man, and the man is the head of a woman, and God is the head of Christ.

Ephesians 5:23

For the husband is the head of the wife, as Christ also is the head of the church, He Himself being the Savior of the body.

I Corinthians 10:31

Whether, then, you eat or drink or whatever you do, do all to the glory of God.

Proverbs 22:3

The prudent sees the evil and hides himself, But the naive go on, and are punished for it.

Proverbs 27:12

A prudent man sees evil and hides himself, The naive proceed and pay the penalty.

I Only Have Eyes For You

II Corinthians 10:5

We are destroying speculations and every lofty thing raised up against the knowledge of God, and we are taking every thought captive to the obedience of Christ,

I Corinthians 13:4

Love is patient, love is kind and is not jealous; love does not brag and is not arrogant,

I Corinthians 13:7

(love)bears all things, believes all things, hopes all things, endures all things.

Oh Be Careful Little Mouth What You Say

Proverbs 31:23

Her husband is known in the gates, When he sits among the elders of the land.

Luke 6:45

"The good man out of the good treasure of his heart brings forth what is good; and the evil man out of the evil treasure brings forth what is evil; for his mouth speaks from that which fills his heart.

Proverbs 10:19

When there are many words, transgression is unavoidable, But he who restrains his lips is wise.

Life Is So Unnerving For a Servant Who's Not Serving

I Peter 3:7

You husbands in the same way, live with your wives in an understanding way, as with someone weaker, since she is a woman; and show her honor as a fellow heir of the grace of life, so that your prayers will not be hindered.

Proverbs 14:1

The wise woman builds her house, But the foolish tears it down with her own hands.

Genesis 2:24

For this reason a man shall leave his father and his mother, and be joined to his wife; and they shall become one flesh.

If you were looking for the "sex verses," I would encourage you to complete the "Spicy" bible study found in our Marriage Matters package or available at Characterhealth.com

James 4:17

Therefore, to one who knows the right thing to do and does not do it, to him it is sin.

Proverbs 3:27

Do not withhold good from those to whom it is due, When it is in your power to do it.

Matthew 7:12

"In everything, therefore, treat people the same way you want them to treat you, for this is the Law and the Prophets."

Do You Really Want To Change?

Proverbs 31:1-31

The words of King Lemuel, the oracle which his mother taught him:
What, O my son?
And what, O son of my womb?
And what, O son of my vows?
Do not give your strength to women,
Or your ways to that which destroys kings.
It is not for kings, O Lemuel,
It is not for kings to drink wine,
Or for rulers to desire strong drink,
For they will drink and forget what is decreed,
And pervert the rights of all the afflicted.
Give strong drink to him who is perishing,
And wine to him whose life is bitter.
Let him drink and forget his poverty

And remember his trouble no more.
Open your mouth for the mute,
For the rights of all the unfortunate.
Open your mouth, judge righteously,
And defend the rights of the afflicted and needy.
An excellent wife, who can find?
For her worth is far above jewels.
The heart of her husband trusts in her,
And he will have no lack of gain.
She does him good and not evil
All the days of her life.
She looks for wool and flax
And works with her hands in delight.
She is like merchant ships;
She brings her food from afar.
She rises also while it is still night
And gives food to her household
And portions to her maidens.
She considers a field and buys it;
From her earnings she plants a vineyard.
She girds herself with strength
And makes her arms strong.
She senses that her gain is good;
Her lamp does not go out at night.
She stretches out her hands to the distaff,
And her hands grasp the spindle.
She extends her hand to the poor,
And she stretches out her hands to the needy.
She is not afraid of the snow for her household,
For all her household are clothed with scarlet.
She makes coverings for herself;
Her clothing is fine linen and purple.

Her husband is known in the gates,
    When he sits among the elders of the land.
She makes linen garments and sells them,
    And supplies belts to the tradesmen.
Strength and dignity are her clothing,
    And she smiles at the future.
She opens her mouth in wisdom,
    And the teaching of kindness is on her tongue.
She looks well to the ways of her household,
    And does not eat the bread of idleness.
Her children rise up and bless her;
    Her husband also, and he praises her, saying:
"Many daughters have done nobly,
    But you excel them all."
Charm is deceitful and beauty is vain,
    But a woman who fears the LORD, she shall be praised.
Give her the product of her hands,
    And let her works praise her in the gates.

Proverbs 25:24

It is better to live in a corner of the roof than in a house shared with a contentious woman.

Ephesians 5:22-24

Wives, be subject to your own husbands, as to the Lord. For the husband is the head of the wife, as Christ also is the head of the church, He Himself being the Savior of the body. But as the church is subject to Christ, so also the wives ought to be to their husbands in everything.

Colossians 3:19

Husbands, love your wives and do not be embittered against them.

I Peter 3:1-6

In the same way, you wives, be submissive to your own husbands so that even if any of them are disobedient to the word, they may be won without a word by the behavior of their wives, as they observe your chaste and respectful behavior. Your adornment must not be merely external—braiding the hair, and wearing gold jewelry, or putting on dresses; but let it be the hidden person of the heart, with the imperishable quality of a gentle and quiet spirit, which is precious in the sight of God. For in this way in former times the holy women also, who hoped in God, used to adorn themselves, being submissive to their own husbands; just as Sarah obeyed Abraham, calling him lord, and you have become her children if you do what is right without being frightened by any fear.

Ephesians 5:25-28

Husbands, love your wives, just as Christ also loved the church and gave Himself up for her, so that He might sanctify her, having cleansed her by the washing of water with the word, that He might present to Himself the church in all her glory, having no spot or wrinkle or any such thing; but that she would be holy and blameless. So husbands ought also to love their own wives as their own bodies. He who loves his own wife loves himself;

James 1:22-24

But prove yourselves doers of the word, and not merely hearers who delude themselves. For if anyone is a hearer of the word and not a doer, he is like a man who looks at his natural face in a mirror; for once he has looked at himself and gone away, he has immediately forgotten what kind of person he was.

Jeremiah 17:9

"The heart is more deceitful than all else And is desperately sick; Who can understand it?"

Ephesians 5:21

And be subject to one another in the fear of Christ.

Give Thanks With a Grateful Heart

Luke 6:38

"Give, and it will be given to you. They will pour into your lap a good measure-- pressed down, shaken together, and running over. For by your standard of measure it will be measured to you in return."

Honoring Your Husband Through Prayer

I Thessalonians 5:17

Pray without ceasing;

Ephesians 5:25-29

Husbands, love your wives, just as Christ also loved the church and gave Himself up for her, so that He might sanctify her, having cleansed her by the washing of water with the word, that He might present to Himself the church in all her glory, having no spot or wrinkle or any such thing; but that she would be holy and blameless. So husbands ought also to love their own wives as their own bodies. He who loves his own wife loves himself; for no one ever hated his own flesh, but nourishes and cherishes it, just as Christ also does the church.

Psalm 46:1

God is our refuge and strength, A very present help in trouble.

James 1:5

But if any of you lacks wisdom, let him ask of God, who gives to all generously and without reproach, and it will be given to him.

Ephesians 1:16-19

Do not cease giving thanks for you, while making mention of you in my prayers; that the God of our Lord Jesus Christ, the Father of glory, may give to you a spirit of wisdom and of revelation in the knowledge of Him. I pray that the eyes of your heart may be enlightened, so that you will know what is the hope of His calling, what are the riches of the glory of His inheritance in the saints, and what is the surpassing greatness of His power toward us who believe. These are in accordance with the working of the strength of His might.

Colossians 1:9-12

For this reason also, since the day we heard of it, we have not ceased to pray for you and to ask that you may be filled with the knowledge of His will in all spiritual wisdom and understanding, so that you will walk in a manner worthy of the Lord, to please Him in all respects, bearing fruit in every good work and increasing in the knowledge of God; strengthened with all power, according to His glorious might, for the attaining of all steadfastness and patience; joyously giving thanks to the Father, who has qualified us to share in the inheritance of the saints in Light.

When Life Isn't Sunshine and Roses

Proverbs 31:17

She girds herself with strength And makes her arms strong.

James 1:2-3

Consider it all joy, my brethren, when you encounter various trials, knowing that the testing of your faith produces endurance. And let endurance have its perfect result, so that you may be perfect and complete, lacking in nothing.

Romans 8:28

And we know that God causes all things to work together for good to those who love God, to those who are called according to His purpose.

I Corinthians 10:31

Whether, then, you eat or drink or whatever you do, do all to the glory of God.

Ephesians 5:22

Wives, be subject to your own husbands, as to the Lord.

Romans 12:18

If possible, so far as it depends on you, be at peace with all men.

I Corinthians 10:13

No temptation has overtaken you but such as is common to man; and God is faithful, who will not allow you to be tempted beyond what you are able, but with the temptation will provide the way of escape also, so that you will be able to endure it.

II Corinthians 10:5

We are destroying speculations and every lofty thing raised up against the knowledge of God, and we are taking every thought captive to the obedience of Christ.

Philippians 4:8

Finally, brethren, whatever is true, whatever is honorable, whatever is right, whatever is pure, whatever is lovely, whatever is of good repute, if there is any excellence and if anything worthy of praise, dwell on these things.

Galatians 6:2

Bear one another's burdens, and thereby fulfill the law of Christ.

Matthew 7:12

"In everything, therefore, treat people the same way you want them to treat you, for this is the Law and the Prophets."

Matthew 25:40

"The King will answer and say to them, 'Truly I say to you, to the extent that you did it to one of these brothers of Mine, even the least of them, you did it to Me.'"

Proverbs 18:14

The spirit of a man can endure his sickness, But as for a broken spirit who can bear it?

Psalm 34:18

The LORD is near to the brokenhearted And saves those who are crushed in spirit.

II Corinthians 12:7

Because of the surpassing greatness of the revelations, for this reason, to keep me from exalting myself, there was given me a thorn in the flesh, a messenger of Satan to torment me-- to keep me from exalting myself!

I Peter 3:1-2

In the same way, you wives, be submissive to your own husbands so that even if any of them are disobedient to the word, they may be won without a word by the behavior of their wives, as they observe your chaste and respectful behavior.

Luke 17:3

"Be on your guard! If your brother sins, rebuke him; and if he repents, forgive him."

James 5:19-20

My brethren, if any among you strays from the truth and one turns him back, let him know that he who turns a sinner from the error of his way will save his soul from death and will cover a multitude of sins.

John 3:19-20

"This is the judgment, that the Light has come into the world, and men loved the darkness rather than the Light, for their deeds were evil."

Galatians 6:1

Brethren, even if anyone is caught in any trespass, you who are spiritual, restore such a one in a spirit of gentleness; each one looking to yourself, so that you too will not be tempted.

Malachi 2:16

"For I hate divorce," says the LORD, the God of Israel, "and him who covers his garment with wrong," says the LORD of hosts. "So take heed to your spirit, that you do not deal treacherously."

Galatians 6:9

Let us not lose heart in doing good, for in due time we will reap if we do not grow weary.

Pushing the Reset Button

Ephesians 4:15-16

But speaking the truth in love, we are to grow up in all aspects into Him who is the head, even Christ, from whom the whole body, being fitted and held together by what every joint supplies, according to the proper working of each individual part, causes the growth of the body for the building up of itself in love.

Ephesians 4:20-24

But you did not learn Christ in this way, if indeed you have heard Him and have been taught in Him, just as truth is in Jesus, that, in reference to your former manner of life, you lay aside the old self, which is being corrupted in accordance with the lusts of deceit, and that you be renewed in the spirit of your mind, and put on the new self, which in the likeness of God has been created in righteousness and holiness of the truth.

James 1:19

This you know, my beloved brethren. But everyone must be quick to hear, slow to speak and slow to anger;

Ephesians 4:26

Be angry, and yet do not sin; do not let the sun go down on your anger.

Matthew 21:12-13

And Jesus entered the temple and drove out all those who were buying and selling in the temple, and overturned the tables of the moneychangers and the seats of those who were selling doves. And He said to them, "It is written, 'My house shall be called a house of prayer'; but you are making it a robbers' den."

John 2:14-17

And He found in the temple those who were selling oxen and sheep and doves, and the moneychangers seated at their tables. And He made a scourge of cords, and drove them all out of the temple, with the sheep and the oxen; and He poured out the coins of the moneychangers and overturned their tables; and to those who were selling the doves He said, "Take these things away; stop making My Father's house a place of business." His disciples remembered that it was written, "Zeal for your house will consume Me."

Jeremiah 17:9

"The heart is more deceitful than all else And is desperately sick; Who can understand it?"

I John 1:9

If we confess our sins, He is faithful and righteous to forgive us our sins and to cleanse us from all unrighteousness.

Wrapping Things Up

Galatians 6:9

Let us not lose heart in doing good, for in due time we will reap if we do not grow weary.

BOOK STUDY GUIDE

I hope you're enjoying The Wise Wife! This book study guide is intended to help you personalize each chapter and truly make it your own. The questions are meant to help you personally evaluate new concepts and spend some time setting new goals.

Growing in our relationship with the Lord and in our role as a wise wife can be challenging! May I encourage you to invite some other ladies to join you on this journey? Plan a time to gather each week in order to spend time discussing each chapter. Every participant should read the assigned chapter and answer the study guide questions for themselves. Preparation ahead of time will set the stage for good discussion and practical brainstorming.

Have fun in your book study group! Enjoy some coffee or tea. Perhaps indulge in cookies, or muffins, or hot fudge sundaes! (My personal recommendation) As you study together, you will be constructing a solid group of like-minded wives who can then encourage and exhort one another when the going gets tough.

The book study questions are introspective and focused on each chapter. For those who desire to go even deeper in their study of marriage and wise living, a complementary Bible study is available at Characterhealth.com. That study would also make a great group study and it will take you on a thorough walk through the scriptures to accompany each chapter you are reading.

I'd love to hear from you about the proactive changes you are making in your marriage! You can always reach me through the "Contact" button at Characterhealth.com. May God bless you as you seek to honor Him through becoming a Wise Wife!

Megan Ann

Chapter One It's Not About The Wedding… It's About The Marriage

This week, the goal is to take a look in the rear view mirror. We'll spend some time considering the expectations with which we entered marriage and how those expectations have shaped our marriage to this day. Also, just for fun, we'll spend some time reminiscing about that "man of our dreams!"

Think About it:

1. What is the strongest memory you have from your wedding day? Record that memory in the space provided, complete with all the gory details…

2. When you met your husband what was the first thing that attracted you to him? What would he say is the first thing that attracted him to you? How has your attraction changed after transitioning from a dating to a married couple?

3. How would you describe your spiritual life as a newlywed? Were you a believer? Were you and your husband equally yoked not only as believers, but also in your biblical worldview and goals for serving the Lord?

4. What was your first area of disagreement as newlyweds? How did you resolve that conflict?

5. Whom do you admire as a practical example of a woman who lives the life of a Wise Wife? What makes that woman different from other women?

6. What would you consider to be your greatest strength as a wife?

7. What would you consider to be your greatest weakness as a wife?

8. What do you hope to learn through this study?

Make It Yours:
Remember that woman you wrote about it question #5? Sit down and write her a note of encouragement. Share the example she has been for you and thank her for faithfully exemplifying how to live as a Wise Wife.

Chapter Two Men and Women: There Really Is a Difference

This week's goal is to help us recognize those situations that propel us into the crazy cycle with our husbands. As well, we'll isolate what behaviors our husbands see as respectful, and those that are received as disrespect.

Think About It:

1. Using only 3 sentences, describe in your own words what you see as the biggest difference between men and women.

2. According to Emerson Eggerichs, what is a woman's greatest need?

3. Again, according to Dr. Eggerichs, what is a man's greatest need?

4. Record one way that your husband fulfills your need for love?

5. What causes you and your husband to get into the crazy cycle? What do you do when this happens?

6. Why should a woman make the choice to respect her husband?

7. On page 28, we are reminded of the need for a certain type of goal for our marriage. What is that goal? How can you remain focused on that goal when your husband does not seem worthy

of respect? Record some practical suggestions that could be helpful to others as well.

8. In your own words, describe what this phrase means to you, "Your marriage is a ministry."

9. Share one example of a trap in which you found yourself in your marriage relationship. Was that trap one that was easily avoided or was it an unseen trap that caught you up unaware?

10. According to what you read, what two actions are necessary if we are going to live wisely?

Make It Yours:

Make a list of words that convey respect to your husband. Using the list as your basis for action, see how many words you can use this week in conversation with him. Pay close attention to how he responds to your respectful communication.

Chapter 3 I Only Have Eyes For You

This week the focus is on learning how to incorporate change in our lives. In the process, we'll examine our own life to determine some areas of needed growth and change.

Think About It:

1. What actions to you show that would help your husband recognize that you are feeling unloved? Does he recognize those actions? In other words, are the actions getting the hoped for response?

2. What actions does your husband show when he is feeling a lack of respect? How do you respond when you see him showing you those actions?

3. According to what you read, how must we readjust our focus if we are going to learn how to effectively respect our husbands?

4. What is the first step necessary if we are going to understand that we need to change our actions and attitude?

5. What are some ways we can come to that realization?

6. According to what you read, simply having an emotional reaction when we realize we must enact change doesn't mean we've actually changed. What must happen for change to become a reality in our lives?

7. Why is praying for God to take away our bad attitude an ineffective means of praying?

8. Time to get honest with yourself. Do you struggle with feelings of spiritual superiority? What causes you to have those feelings and what will you do to change your attitude?

9. Is there any activity, in which you are involved, (i.e. social media, television viewing, etc.) that threatens to draw your heart away from your husband? If so, what practical action steps will you take to disarm that temptation?

10. Why is it so important to allow your husband to fail?

Make It Yours:

Rather than worry about her husband's spiritual growth, a wise wife will be committed to personal growth and change. Make a list of practical ways you will incorporate in order to grow deeper in your own walk with the Lord.

Chapter Four Oh Be Careful Little Mouth What You Say

Shhh! This week's goal is to begin the process of taming that unruly tongue of ours! We'll look at how to change our communication from hurtful to full of blessing. Just for fun, we'll record some of those "sweet" pet names we use to describe our husbands!

Think About It:

1. According to what you read, our words have the power to do one of two things. What are those two things?

2. Think back over the last 24 hours and the communication you had with your husband during that time. Were your words characterized by a desire to build him up or were they words meant to wound and destroy?

3. Why is what we say about our husbands to other people so important? What is at stake by what we say?

4. What does the word sarcasm literally mean? Has anyone ever said something to you sarcastically that left a gaping wound?

5. Where does what comes out of our mouths actually originate? Understanding that our hearts dictate our speech, what are three practical steps you can take to make sure your speech is biblical and uplifting?

6. What does the word "encourage" mean? Record the last encouraging thing you said to your husband.

7. According to what you read, what is one tool to assist you when it is time to bring up a difficult conversation?

8. How do good questions help us to avoid defensiveness?

9. Do you have a "brutally effective trigger word?" How does your husband respond when you pull that word out of your arsenal? How can you remind yourself to not use that expression or word? Be specific and list at least one practical idea to squash that word or expression and erase it from your vocabulary.

10. I'm an eye-roller. What negative non-verbal cues do you use to express your displeasure to your husband? How does he respond to those cues?

11. Just for fun… what "sweet" pet names do you use to refer to your husband? What names does he have for you?

Make It Yours:

This will take some courage! Go to your husband and ask him if there is any expression or word you use that escalates strife between the two of you. In the same manner, ask him to describe any non-verbal actions you use to express displeasure or disrespect. Take a deep breath and pray for God to help you hate those words or actions!

Chapter Five Life Is So Unnerving For a Servant Who's Not Serving

Get ready to exercise those muscles! This week is all about learning to serve and serve with a joyful heart. It's time to stretch out and go beyond what's easy... Let's find some new ways to bless our husbands!

Think About It:

1. In your own words, describe what it means for a wife to, "build her own home."

2. Why is marriage the only permanent relationship according to the scriptures? What does it mean to leave and cleave?

3. When was the last time you went out on a date with your husband? What did you do on your date?

4. List three "girlfriend" expressions of affection you can show your husband this week. Then, put them into action!

5. When was the last time you and your husband went away for an overnight? If it's never happened, or if it's been a long time, is it because you were uncomfortable leaving. What can you do to make an overnight possible?

6. Is there anything that is causing stress in your sexual relationship? What can you do to make sex a priority in your marriage?

7. According to what you read, what happens when we refuse to accept our husband's evaluation of our beauty and worth?

8. What makes your husband different from other men? Considering those differences, how can you serve him in ways that are uniquely suited to his specific needs? Make a list of practical ideas.

9. Is there any specific way you serve your husband that other ladies notice? How can you use that service to point to Jesus?

10. According to what you read, what is the goal of the bigger picture in serving our husbands?

Make It Yours:
Sometimes we spend inordinate amounts of time serving our husbands in ways that are not important to them. In order to be a good steward of your time and resources, ask your husband what acts of service he finds to be the most meaningful. Make those acts of service your priority this week and observe his reaction.

Chapter Six Do You Really Want To Change?

Like her, love her, or hate her this week we'll spend some time looking at the life of the Proverbs 31 woman. The biggest question we'll answer this week is "Do you really want to change?" While Proverbs 31 certainly isn't a to-do list that we must follow in order to be spiritual, the life of the Proverbs 31 woman does provide food for thought as we consider how to live wisely in our marriages.

Think About It:

1. Be honest, what is the first thing that comes to mind when you consider the Proverbs 31 woman?

2. To whom was Proverbs 31 written? Why does it matter?

3. In your own words, describe what it means for an excellent wife to be "found."

4. What practical things would you like your husband to do as he provides an atmosphere for you to grow in your role as his wife? Make a list of those things that would be helpful and share the list with your husband.

5. How do you respond when your husband attempts to challenge an area of needed growth in your life?

6. According to what you read, what four steps can we take in order to learn to listen to our husbands more effectively?

7. What negative character quality keeps us from thankfully receiving instruction from our husbands? What positive character quality must we cultivate in order to be eager learners?

8. In your own words, explain why God gave your children two parents? Write a purpose statement regarding how you will respond when your husband parents the children in a way that is different than how you would do it.

9. Has your husband encouraged you to pursue any specific gift or talent he sees in your life? What is that gift or talent?

10. List five practical ways you will seek to develop your unique talents in order to be used more effectively by the Lord.

Make It Yours:

Spend some time in prayer asking the Lord to show you areas of opportunity for service. As you begin to recognize new ways to serve, seek your husband's counsel and ask him if he sees those areas as possible new avenues of ministry for you.

Chapter Seven Give Thanks With a Grateful Heart

A thankful heart will make the hardest service joyful. A thankful heart will change our attitude and refocus our troubled heart. A thankful heart is a contented heart. This week's study is all about becoming those thankful women of God that radiate joy and draw others to the Savior!

Think About It:

1. Consider the quote, "Gratitude is the memory of the heart." What are some memories that fill your heart with grateful thanksgiving?

2. When was the last time you paused in the midst of your busyness to simply consider all of the things for which you can be thankful. Quickly compile a list of 10 things that produce thankfulness in your heart.

3. Consider your communication with your husband within the last 24 hours. During your times of communication, did you communicate that you are content and thankful? Did you communicate that he hasn't provided all that you need? Don't hurry over this answer… Sometimes we don't even realize the message we are sending through our words and it is helpful to slow down and really consider what we are saying.

4. In your own words, describe how contentment and thankfulness go hand in hand.

5. According to what your read, to what are contentment and thankfulness directly related?

6. What message do we communicate to our husbands when we are careful stewards of what they have provided for us?

7. Do you thank your husband verbally for the ways he provides for you? Make a list of 5 ways your husband provides for you and find a way to thank him for each of those areas this week.

8. What little things does your husband do simply because he loves you and want to lighten your load? Make a list of those things!

9. What are some areas of protection your husband has provided that have kept you from harm?

10. Every husband is unique and they each have their own special quirks and oddities. Is there an area of your husband's life that you struggle to be thankful for on a daily basis. Write a one-sentence statement affirming that you will strive to be thankful for your husband just the way he is and with no changes necessary!

Make It Yours:

Spend one hour making a comprehensive list of everything for which you are thankful. Include everything about your husband that incites gratitude in your heart. Share the list with your husband and ask him to add to it.

Chapter Eight Honoring Your Husband Through Prayer

What a precious privilege we have to take our husbands and their needs before the throne of God! Prayer is our most valuable asset as we seek to love our husbands and minister to them with wisdom. The goal this week is to make prayer our first action step as we seek to live as Wise Wives.

Think About It:

1. In your own words, describe what it means to "Pray without Ceasing."

2. Why is it important as we pray for our husbands to begin with praying for ourselves?

3. According to what you read, what is the first thing that is changed by prayer?

4. Have you ever found yourself praying that God would just change your husband? What was the outcome of those prayers?

5. If we are praying that our husbands will faithfully follow God's will for their lives, it may mean that our lives will change dramatically. How can you prepare you heart to welcome whatever God calls your husband to do, regardless of the outcome for you?

6. Why do our husbands need an extra measure of discernment?

7. How easy is it for your husband to find the time he needs to interact with the Word of God? What practical steps can you take to make it easier for him to have this time?

8. Is there any part of your husband's life that is too small or inconsequential to take to God in prayer?

9. What is your first avenue of help if your husband doesn't want to pray with you?

10. What part do the scriptures play regarding how we pray for our husbands?

Make It Yours:
Get a notebook and begin keeping a list of areas about which you are praying for your husband. Ask him for specific prayer requests and joyfully remind him when God has answered those prayers.

Chapter Nine When Life Isn't Sunshine and Roses

This week deals with some hard issues. Take your time and carefully consider your answers to the questions provided. If you are doing this study in a small group, practice wisdom as you share your answers.

Think About It:

1. Why is it important to understand our own need for change before we ever consider areas of sin in our husband's life?

2. What role do boring and mundane days play in our lives?

3. As Christians, should we be surprised when trials come into our lives?

4. What is the purpose of trials and what should our goal be as we endure trials?

5. As you consider that trials are for our good and God's glory, what is our responsibility in that equation?

6. What are some practical steps you can take in order to bring glory to God during a time of trial?

7. Have your in-laws ever been the cause of strife in your marriage? How did you handle that strife?

8. In your own words, describe what Romans 12:18 means when it says, "If possible, so far as it depends on you, be at peace with all men."

9. Has your husband ever faced unemployment? What did you do to help him during that time? If your husband hasn't faced this issue, think about what you could proactively do should the situation arise.

10. Consider and compare how you like to be treated during a time of illness and how your husband likes to be treated. What are the differences in your desires?

11. Has your husband dealt with depression? What are some practical steps a wife can take to minister to her husband during such a time?

Make It Your Own:

If your husband has brought the trial of unrepentant sin into your home, make a practical plan to address the sin. Pray and prepare your heart to forgive him and restore with him. Consider whom you will seek out for godly counsel if necessary. If a husband in sin is not an issue in your home, praise God and pray for your husband to continue to walk faithfully with Him.

Chapter Ten Pushing the Reset Button

Although it's toward the end of the book, this week's study may very well be the most important chapter of the book. Every marriage will encounter times of strife and difficulty. Learning how to effectively seek and offer forgiveness will heal the wounds caused by those difficult times.

Think About It:

1. In your own words, describe what this quote means, "To remain static as a Christian is to commit spiritual suicide."

2. Why is it important to practice both sides of the put-off/put-on principle?

3. According to what you read, what is ultimately the purpose of growing and changing?

4. According to the book of James, what must we be quick to do if we truly desire to live wisely?

5. What is the best response we can give our husbands when they point out needful areas of change?

6. In your own words, describe the difference between apology and seeking forgiveness.

7. What must we recognize in order to repent?

8. Why is it so important to deal with even the mildest irritation in our relationship with our husband?

9. With whom must we begin when we are seeking forgiveness?

10. Forgiveness, when coupled with restoration provides what for our relationship with our husband?

11. When was the last time you sought your husband's forgiveness? Are there issues that need the medicine of forgiveness to heal the wounds that are lingering in your marriage?

Make It Yours:
This week, spend time in prayer asking the Lord to reveal any areas in your marriage that need to be addressed by seeking forgiveness. Be thorough in your prayer and as the Holy Spirit reveals areas be quick to act!

Chapter Eleven Wrapping Things Up

This week is a catchall; it's an opportunity to look back over what you've learned and make a deep commitment to God-honoring change. Just learning about becoming a wise wife is never enough. Until we take that head knowledge and make it applicable through practical actions, we are no better off than when we began. My prayer is that you will walk away from this study better equipped to love and serve your husband by choosing to live as a Wise Wife.

Think About It:

1. What is the biggest "new" truth you've learned in the last ten weeks?

2. How will you put that "new" truth into action?

3. What is the most surprising thing you learned regarding what men consider respectful or disrespectful?

4. What new practices have you put into place in order to live more wisely?

5. Has your husband noticed any changes in the way you are living? If so, what has he said about those changes?

6. What changes will you incorporate that will effectively push you outside of your comfort zone?

7. After spending ten weeks considering how you can change in order to glorify God and honor your husband are you less prone to focus on his areas of weakness?

8. Have you begun to resolve even the mildest irritations in your marriage? What has been the fruit of that change?

9. In which area do you think God is most clearly calling you to change your attitudes and actions?

10. What are the only two reasons that will keep us moving forward and looking upward as we seek to become Wise Wives?

Make It Yours:
Change is an absolutely necessary part of every believer's life. In a notebook, make two columns. Label one column, "Put-off" and label the other column, "Put-on." Keep a running list of the areas in which God, through the Holy Spirit, reminds you of the need to change. Refer back to your notebook often and rejoice as you see Christ-like change occurring in your life!

BIOGRAPHY OF MEGAN SCHEIBNER

Megan was born March 13th 1962 and came home to her adoptive family March 15th. She grew up in York, PA and graduated from York Suburban H.S. in 1980. Four years later, she earned a B.A. in Speech Communications from West Chester University. She uses her degree as she teaches and speaks at conferences and women's ministry functions, as well as in individual and couples counseling.

Megan is the home schooling mother of eight beautiful children, four boys and four girls. She has been married for 29 years to her college sweetheart, Steve Scheibner. Together they have co-authored Parenting Matters, The Nine Practices of the Pro-Active Parent. She is also the author of a series of discipleship books for mothers and several devotional Bible studies. She authored, "In My Seat," the story of Steve's 9/11 experience, that has captivated millions on YouTube. Her newest book, "An A-Z Guide For Character-Healthy Homeschooling" provides encouragement and practical tips gained through her 20 plus years of homeschooling experience. She is a popular speaker, guest on Family Talk with Dr. James Dobson, and TV personality on the Glenn Beck TV show.

Megan and her husband Steve share a strong desire to equip today's parents to raise the next generation of character healthy leaders. In her spare time, she loves to run and play tennis. Megan enjoys writing, cooking, feeding teenagers, reading, and everything pertaining to the Boston Red Sox.

Books by Megan:

- Character Matters: A Daily Step-By-Step Guide To Developing Courageous Character
- Eight Rules of Communication For Successful Marriages
- An A-Z Guide For Character-Healthy Homeschooling
- In My Seat: A Pilot's Story From Sept.10th-11th.
- Grand Slam: A Four Week Devotional Bible Study For Christian Athletes.
- Rise and Shine: Recipes and Routines For Your Morning.
- Lunch and Literature.
- Dinner and Discipleship.
- Studies in Character.
- The King of Thing and The Kingdom of Thingdom.
- Talk Time: 60 Days of Devotional Thoughts to Make Your Marriage Rock.